Volume A

Focus on Grammar

WORKBOOK

A

HIGH-INTERMEDIATE
Course for
Reference
and Practice

Marjorie Fuchs

Margaret Bonner

Longman

**Focus on Grammar: A High-Intermediate Course
for Reference and Practice Workbook, Volume A**

Editorial Director: Joanne Dresner
Development Editor: Nancy Perry
Production Editor: Carol Harwood
Text Design Adaptation: Circa 86
Cover Design: A Good Thing, Inc.

ISBN 0-201-82582-1

5 6 7 8 9 10 - CRS - 98

Contents

About the Authors

Marjorie Fuchs taught ESL for eight years at New York City Technical College and LaGuardia Community College of the City University of New York, and EFL at the Sprach Studio Lingua Nova in Munich, Germany. She has authored and co-authored many widely used ESL textbooks, notably *On Your Way, Crossroads, Top Twenty ESL Word Games, Around the World: Pictures for Practice, Families: Ten Card Games for Language Learners, Focus on Grammar: An Intermediate Course for Reference and Practice,* and the *Workbooks* to the *Longman Dictionary of American English, The Longman Photo Dictionary,* and the *Vistas* series.

Margaret Bonner has been teaching and writing since 1978. She has taught at Hunter College, the Borough of Manhattan Community College, the National Taiwan University, and the Center for International Programs at Virginia Commonwealth University. Currently she is teaching at John Tyler Community College in Midlothian, Virginia. She worked for three years as a textbook author for the school system of the Sultanate of Oman, and she contributed to the *On Your Way* series and *Focus on Grammar: An Intermediate Course for Reference and Practice.* Her most recent text is *Step into Writing.*

UNIT 1

Review and Integration: Present, Past, Present Perfect

1. Spelling: Simple Present Tense and Present Progressive

Complete the chart.

BASE FORM	THIRD-PERSON SINGULAR	PRESENT PARTICIPLE
1. answer	answers	answering
2. ask	asks	
3. begin	begins	beginning
4. bite	bits	bitting
5. buy	buys	buying
6. come	comes	coming
7. dig	digs	digging
8. do	does	doing
9. enjoy	employs	employing
10. fly	flies	flying
11. forget	forgets	forgetting
12. have	has	having
13. lie	lies	lying
14. manage		
15.		promising
16.	says	
17. study		
18.		traveling
19. use		
20.	writes	

2. Contrast: Simple Present Tense or Present Progressive

Complete the article with the simple present tense or present progressive form of the verbs in parentheses.

Right now Pat O'Neil ____*is taking*____ a test, but she _____
1. (take)   2. (not know)

it. She _____ on what she _____, not on how. The person
3. (concentrate)   4. (write)

who _____ her the test is not a teacher. He's a graphologist—a person
5. (give)

who _____ handwriting. Graphologists _____ that
6. (study)   7. (believe)

the way people _____ _____ something about their personality and character.
8. (write)   9. (tell)

At first I was skeptical, but now, after reading several books and attending a workshop,

I _____ to believe that there might be something to it after all. According
10. (begin)

to graphologist Andrea McNichol, most people _____ graphology very
11. (not take)

seriously in the United States, but much of the rest of the world _____ it
12. (find)

indispensable.

One graphologist, Huntington Hartford, author of *You Are What You Write,*

always _____ his "victims" to write a variation of the sentence
13. (ask)

"I _____ down the street to get the horse and buggy out of the carriage
14. (walk)

house." Hartford _____ that he _____ how the
15. (say)   16. (not remember)

sentence started. He _____, however, that its purpose is to include as
17. (know)

many letters of the alphabet as possible. The test takers always _____ a
18. (use)

fountain pen or a pencil (never a ball-point), and Hartford _____
19. (tell)

them not to worry about spelling.

Now Pat O'Neil _____ a similar sentence to a personnel clerk, who
20. (hand)

will turn it over to a graphologist. What _____ the graphologist

_____ to learn from Pat's sample? To find out, we talked to Perry Bland,
21. (hope)

the graphology consultant in the company Pat O'Neil _____ to join.
22. (want)

"In Pat's sample, I _____ for tendencies to act in certain ways,"
23. (look)

explained Bland. "I _____ the slant of her writing and its position on the
24. (examine)

page, among other things. For example, a left slant usually _____ a
25. (indicate)

somewhat withdrawn personality." He showed us an anonymous sample. "This

person _____ through a very difficult time at the moment, and
26. (go)

he _____ it very well. But he _____ in anyone.
27. (handle)   28. (not confide)

His writing _____ this tendency very clearly.
29. (show)

"The right-hand margin of the page _____ the future," continued
30. (represent)

Bland. "Here's a writing sample from an executive who right now _____
31. (plan)

a new direction for a large company. Notice that this person _____
32. (not leave)

much room in the right-hand margin. This is the writing of someone who never

_____ looking at the future."
33. (avoid)

"What about signatures?" I asked. "Yes, signatures _____
34. (tell)

us a lot about someone," Bland affirmed. "Look at this one by a chief executive officer of a

large firm. You _____ about him in the news these days because the
35. (read)

government _____ his company. Those large, unnecessary
36. (investigate)

strokes _____ his showy personality. Here's a person who
37. (display)

_____ his own achievements and _____ advantage
38. (emphasize)   39. (take)

of other people."

Bland always _____, however, that his analysis
40. (warn)

_____ an applicant's future performance. Careful review of a complete
41. (not guarantee)

application is required–and that's no crystal ball either.

3. Spelling: Regular and Irregular Simple Past Tense Forms

Complete the chart.

BASE FORM	PAST TENSE
1. _agree_	agreed
2. _____	applied
3. be	_____ OR _____
4. become	_____
5. describe	_____
6. develop	_____
7. _____	ate
8. get	_____
9. grow	_____
10. invent	_____
11. live	_____
12. _____	paid
13. permit	_____
14. plan	_____
15. _____	sent
16. sleep	_____

4. Contrast: Simple Past Tense, Past Progressive, or *Was/Were Going To*

Complete this excerpt from a book about graphology. Use the verbs in parentheses and choose the simple past tense, past progressive, or **was/were going to.**

The signers of the Declaration of Independence ___*were risking*___ their lives when they
1. (risk)

_____ this famous document—at that point, they _____ the outcome of the
2. (sign)   3. (not know)

Revolution. What can these famous signatures tell us about their characters?

John Hancock's _____ so large and elaborate that "John Hancock" soon
4. (be)

_____ another word for "signature." The signature, with its loops and underlines,
5. (become)

_____ typical of Hancock, who always _____ attention. Once, while the young
6. (be)   7. (want)

John Hancock _____ in London, his uncle _____ him a letter to scold him for
8. (live)   9. (send)

his extravagance. "I am not remarkable for the plainness of my dress," _____ the nephew,
10. (admit)

who _____ gold lace. When his uncle _____, Hancock _____, at 27, the
11. (love)   12. (die)   13. (become)

richest man in Massachusetts. He _____ his money to resist English dominance. One day,
14. (use)

while an English tax collector _____ one of Hancock's ships, a sailor _____ the
15. (inspect)   16. (push)

official into a cabin and _____ the door shut. In 1775, King George _____ Hancock
17. (nail)   18. (name)

the Most Dangerous American. Hancock _____ Dolly Quincy that spring, but he
19. (marry)

_____ into hiding instead to escape arrest. He _____ in Lexington when the
20. (go)   21. (hide)

first battle of the Revolution _____ there.
22. (begin)

Franklin, another powerful personality, also _____ his name with strong
23. (write)

underlines. The more graceful lines and artistic loops of his signature indicate the creativity and

graciousness of this writer, inventor, and ambassador.

While Franklin _____ as an apprentice in his brother James's print shop,
24. (serve)

he _____ to write for the newspapers, using the pen name Mrs. Silence Dogood. He
25. (start)

_____ only a teenager at the time. James _____ Ben manager of the shop, but he
26. (be)   27. (appoint)

had to change his plans when Ben _____ to Philadelphia to escape James, who
28. (run away)

overworked and even beat him.

While he _____ his own printing business in Philadelphia, Franklin _____
29. (develop)   30. (invent)

the Franklin stove and _____ writing his famous *Poor Richard's Almanack*.
31. (begin)

When trouble _____ with England, Franklin, by then an aging man,
32. (break out)

_____ there to represent the interests of the colonies. In 1775, just before the war,
33. (move)

he _____ a ship to return home. He _____ back to Philadelphia when the
34. (board)   35. (travel)

colonists _____ the first shots of the Revolution, on April 19, 1775.
36. (fire)

5. Spelling: Simple Past Tense and Present Perfect

Complete the chart.

BASE FORM	PAST TENSE	PAST PARTICIPLE
1. become	*became*	*become*
2. bring		
3. choose		
4. delay		
5. feel		
6. find		
7. finish		
8. get		
9. graduate		
10. hide		
11. move		
12. notice		
13. own		
14. read		
15. reply		
16. rip		
17. show		
18. speak		
19. throw		
20. wonder		

6. Contrast: Simple Past Tense, Present Perfect, and Present Perfect Progressive

Look at the reporter's notes about the bride's and the groom's families. Then write sentences about them, using the words in parentheses. Choose the simple past tense, present perfect, or present perfect progressive form of the verbs.

Bride	Groom
Nakisha Skoap	Simon Pohlig
born in Broadfield	moved to Broadfield, 1988
lived here all her life	bought Sharney's Restaurant in 1990
B.A., Claremont College, 1990	author, *Simon Says* and *Duck Soup*,
1987—Began working for	kids' cookbooks
Broadfield Examiner	in Jan., started developing local
1993—became crime news reporter	TV show
started research on articles on crime	Mother—Tina Pohlig, president of
in schools in Jan.	TLC Meals, Inc. for two
Father—James Skoap, joined the	years, but plans to retire soon
Broadfield Police Department	
in 1975, retired in 1995	

1. (Nakisha Skoap/live in Broadfield/all her life)

   Nakisha Skoap has lived in Broadfield all her life.

2. (she/graduate/from college/1990)

   _____

3. (report/crime news/1993)

   _____

4. (recently/research/articles about crime in schools)

   _____

5. (her father/work/for the Broadfield Police Department/twenty years)

   _____

(continued on next page)

6. (Simon Pohlig/move/to Broadfield/1988)

_____

7. (own/Sharney's Restuarant/1990)

_____

8. (write/two cookbooks for children)

_____

9. (plan/TV show/several months)

_____

10. (the groom's mother/serve as/president, TLC Meals, Inc./two years)

_____

7. Integration

Look at Nakisha's job application. Then complete the personnel officer's notes, using the words in parentheses. Choose affirmative or negative forms of the simple present tense, present progressive, simple past tense, past progressive, present perfect, present perfect progressive, or **was/were going to.**

CODEX MAGAZINES JOB APPLICATION

1. Position applied for ___ **Editor** ___   Today's Date: **Nov. 12, 1995**

2. Full legal name ___ **Skoap -Pohlig** **Nakisha**   **Ann**
    Last   First   Middle

3. Current address ___ **22 East 10th Street**

___ **Broadfield,**   **Ohio**   **43216** ___   How long at this address? ___ **5 months**
   City   State   Zip Code

4. Previous address ___ **17 Willow Terrace**

___ **Broadfield,**   **Ohio**   **43216** ___ How long at this address? ___ **1968 - June 1, 1995**
   City   State   Zip Code

5. Education. Circle the number of years of post high school education. 1 2 3 4 5 6 ⑦ 8

6.   Name of Institution   Degree   Major   Dates Attended

   1. **Claremont College**   **B.A.**   **Journalism**   **1986 - 1990**

   2. **Ohio State University**   **——**   **Urban Studies**   **1992**

   3. **Ohio State University**   **Political Science**   **1993 - present**

If you expect to complete an educational program soon, indicate the date and type of program.
I expect to receive my M.S. in Political Science in January.

7. Current job. May we contact your present supervisor? _____ yes ___ **X** ___ no

   Job Title **Reporter**   Employer **Broadfield Examiner**

   Type of Business **newspaper**   Address **1400 River Street, Broadfield, OH 43216**

   Dates (month/year) **9/87** to (month/year) **present**

8. In your own handwriting, describe your duties and what you find most satisfying in this job.

   I am currently a crime reporter for a daily newspaper. I write
   local crime news. I especially enjoy working with my supervisor.

1. Nakisha Skoap-Pohlig _____*wants*_____ to work for Codex as an editor.
   (want)

2. Currently, she _____ as a reporter for a daily newspaper.
   (work)

3. She _____ crime news there.
   (cover)

4. She _____ to be a reporter anymore.
   (want)

5. It appears that she _____ coffee while she _____ the job application.
   (drink)   (make out)

6. As you can see, she _____ some coffee while she _____.
   (spill)   (write)

7. At first, she _____ only her maiden name on the application.
   (write)

8. Then she _____ to write her married name, and she _____ it in between
   (remember)   (squeeze)
   her first name and last name.

9. She _____ at the *Broadfield Examiner* for a long time.
   (work)

10. She _____ her job there while she _____ college.
    (find)   (attend)

11. She _____ at Willow Terrace most of her life.
    (live)

12. At present, she _____ on East 10th Street.
    (live)

13. She probably _____ there when she _____ married.
    (move)   (get)

14. She _____ a Master's Degree in Urban Studies at Ohio State University, but she
    (get)
    _____ her major after a year.
    (change)

15. While she _____ at Ohio State University, she _____ to major in Political Science.
    (study)   (decide)

16. She _____ with her B.A. in 1990.
    (graduate)

17. She _____ her Master's degree yet.
    (receive)

18. The handwriting sample _____ several things about this applicant.
    (show)

19. In question eight of the application, she _____ a space between some words
    (leave)
    when she _____ her supervisor.
    (mention)

20. Maybe she _____ the truth about their relationship on the form.
    (tell)

21. At the moment, she _____ Codex to contact her supervisor.
    (want)

22. In her sample for question eight, she _____ most of the letters, and she _____
    (connect)   (slant)
    her writing either to the left or to the right.

23. These two factors usually _____ clear and independent thinking.
    (indicate)

24. The applicant _____ to be very intelligent.
    (seem)

25. I strongly _____ contacting this applicant for an interview.
    (suggest)

2

Past Perfect

▼

1. Spelling: Regular and Irregular Past Participles

Complete the chart.

BASE FORM	PAST PARTICIPLE
1. do	*done*
2. *fight*	fought
3. entertain	_____
4. cut	_____
5. tell	_____
6. _____	withdrawn
7. practice	_____
8. worry	_____
9. _____	sought
10. sweep	_____
11. quit	_____
12. lead	_____
13. _____	written
14. steal	_____
15. plan	_____
16. _____	broken
17. swim	_____
18. bet	_____
19. _____	sunk
20. forgive	_____

2. Affirmative and Negative Statements

Complete the information about late-night TV talk-show host David Letterman.
Use the past perfect form of the verbs in parentheses and choose between
affirmative and negative.

the
late show
with LETTERMAN

Late-night TV host David Letterman has been described as an "observational comic," famous for his wry comments on everyday life. Even as a young child, Letterman ___had shown___ natural comedic
1. (show)
abilities, entertaining family and friends in his home state of Indiana. Family has always been important to Letterman. His father died when Letterman was twenty-seven. They _____ a close
2. (enjoy)
relationship, and Letterman felt the loss deeply. To this day he remains very attached to the rest of his family—his two sisters and his mother (who occasionally appears on his show).

After getting his degree in radio and TV broadcasting at Ball State University, Letterman worked as a TV announcer and radio talk-show host. Once he substituted for a television weatherman but left after only two weeks because he _____ bored and
3. (become)
_____ to draw objects
4. (start)
in the clouds. He _____ even _____ disasters in
5. (invent)
cities that didn't exist. Letterman was fired. The network _____ his creative
6. (appreciate)
reporting.

In 1975, Letterman left for Los Angeles, armed with six TV

(continued on next page)

comedy scripts he _____.
7. (write)
No one was interested in them.
Letterman began performing at
various comedy clubs. In 1977, he
was hired as a writer and performer
on a variety show. That same
year, he got divorced from his
college sweetheart, to whom he
_____ married for nine
8. (be)
years.

Letterman continued doing
stand-up comedy. Soon he was
discovered by one of Johnny
Carson's talent scouts, who
_____ him perform on
9. (see)
the short-lived TV comedy, "Mary."
Carson, the "king" of late-night TV,
first invited Letterman to appear on
his program, "The Tonight Show," in
November 1978. Although Letterman
_____ late-night TV
10. (do)
before, he quickly became Carson's
most frequent guest host.

Two years later, Letterman got
his own show, which went on the air

at 10:00 A.M. Although the show
_____ favorable
11. (get)
reviews, it was canceled after only
eighteen weeks. The ratings
_____ high, perhaps
12. (be)
because the morning time slot was
wrong for Letterman's kind of
audience.

In 1982, Letterman found the
right show at the right time–his own
"Late Night with David Letterman,"
directly following Carson's "The
Tonight Show." Later, when Carson
announced his plans to retire, a
rivalry to take over "The Tonight
Show" developed between Letterman
and his friend, comedian Jay Leno.
By the time Carson actually left, the
struggle _____ to the
13. (grow)
point where it was dominating both
entertainment and business news.
Network TV _____
14. (see)
anything like it before.

When "The Tonight Show" was
finally offered to Leno, Letterman

switched networks. He _____ it clear to NBC
15. (make)
that he would accept nothing less than the job as host of "The Tonight Show." Letterman signed a contract with CBS for a reported $14 million a year and got his own show, "The Late Show with David Letterman." "I _____ to terms with
16. (come)
the idea of coming to CBS because I did not believe there was anything NBC could do to keep me where I was," Letterman said during an interview. "The Late Show" plays opposite Leno's "The Tonight Show" and so far has gotten higher ratings—giving the last laugh to Letterman, after all.

3. Yes/No Questions and Short Answers

Look at David Letterman's schedule. Ask and answer questions about it.

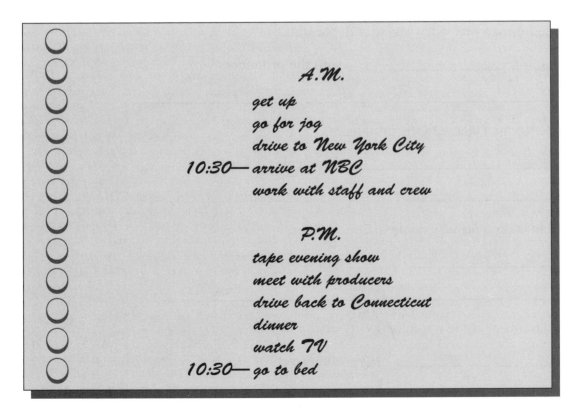

A.M.

get up
go for jog
drive to New York City
10:30— arrive at NBC
work with staff and crew

P.M.

tape evening show
meet with producers
drive back to Connecticut
dinner
watch TV
10:30— go to bed

Source: Based on information from Caroline Latham, "Does Anyone Know the Real David Letterman?" *Cosmopolitan,* January 1987.

1. It was 11:00 A.M.

   A: _____*Had he gotten up*_____ yet?

   B: _____*Yes, he had.*_____

2. Letterman was going for his morning jog.

   A: _____ to New York yet?

   B: _____

3. It was 9:00 A.M.

   A: _____ at NBC by then?

   B: _____

4. It was noon.

   A: _____ for a jog yet?

   B: _____

5. It was late afternoon.

   A: _____ with his staff and crew by then?

   B: _____

6. At 1:00 Letterman was still working with his staff.

   A: _____ with the producers yet?

   B: _____

7. At 6:00 Letterman met with the producers.

   A: _____ the evening show yet?

   B: _____

8. Letterman was on his way home to Connecticut.

   A: _____ dinner yet?

   B: _____

9. Letterman was at home watching TV.

   A: _____ dinner yet?

   B: _____

10. "Late Night" was on TV at 12:30 A.M.

A: _____ to bed yet?

B: _____

4. Simple Past Tense and Past Perfect in Time Clauses

Jay Leno is another late-night TV talk-show host. This timeline shows some important events in his life.

born in New York City

      moved to
      Massachusetts

wrote for TV show "Good Times"

appeared on "Late Night with David Letterman"

appeared in New York comedy clubs

played at Carnegie Hall

graduated from college

did first prime-time TV show

1977

1993

1950

got part-time job as car mechanic

moved to Los Angeles

appeared on "The Tonight Show"

had TV comedy special

got married

became permanent host of "The Tonight Show"

Use the timeline to determine the correct order of the events below. Then combine the phrases, using the past perfect to express the event that occurred first.

1. moved to Massachusetts/graduated from college

By the time *he graduated from college, he had moved to Massachusetts.*

2. appeared in New York City comedy clubs/got a part-time job as a car mechanic

Before _____

3. moved to Los Angeles/wrote for TV

_____ after _____

4. appeared on "The Tonight Show"/wrote for the TV show "Good Times"

By the time _____

(continued on next page)

5. appeared on "The Tonight Show"/appeared on "Late Night with David Letterman"

_____ before _____

6. got married/appeared on "Late Night with David Letterman"

When _____ already _____

7. did his first prime-time TV show/played at Carnegie Hall

By the time _____

8. had a TV comedy special/did his first prime-time TV show

_____ by the time _____

9. became the permanent host of "The Tonight Show"/appeared on "The Tonight Show" many times

_____ when _____

1. Affirmative Statements

Complete the article about jockey Julie Krone. Use the past perfect progressive form of the verbs in parentheses.

June 6, 1993

New York—Julie Krone made horse-racing history yesterday when she won the Belmont Stakes, riding Colonial Affairs. The Belmont Stakes is one of the three Crown races, competitions in which only three women had ever competed before Krone. No woman had won before yesterday.

Krone made her big move about halfway through yesterday's grueling one-and-a-half-mile race. Up to that point, Krone ___*had been worrying*___ 1. (worry) about Sea Hero, but she

_____ Colonial 2. (keep) Affairs at a comfortable pace in the middle of the pack. This was the strategy she and the trainer had agreed on before the race. By the halfway point, Krone and her mount _____ 3. (wait)

and _____ for 4. (hold back) as long as possible. Krone

_____ both 5. (talk to) herself and her horse, trying to keep them both patient. Then at the 3/8 marker, jockey Jerry Bailey started to move Sea Hero out, and Krone exploded into action as well. Unknown to Krone, Sea Hero _____ 6. (run) poorly since a quarter of the way through the race, and Colonial Affairs soon left him in the dust. The crowd, which

_____ "Julie! 7. (shout) Julie!" since Krone's big move at the halfway point, went crazy as she charged into the lead and finished more than two lengths ahead of Kissin Kris, her closest competitor.

Krone's victory was marred somewhat by the

(continued on next page)

accident that befell Prairie Bayou, the expected winner. It _____, and the
8. (rain)
track was slippery. Before the accident, the star thoroughbred _____
9. (gallop)
comfortably along in the back of the pack. Suddenly, he slipped and fell. He was removed from the track by ambulance.

Even before her triumph yesterday, Krone had set records. Before Krone, women had ridden in other Crown races, but no woman had ever entered Belmont Stakes, considered the toughest of the Crown races. By the time she crossed the finish line yesterday, Krone _____ at
10. (compete)
Belmont for two years, a record in itself. Yesterday, she became not only the first woman to compete in this classic race, but the first to win.

2. Questions and Answers

Complete the conversations with the past perfect progressive form of the verbs in parentheses or with short answers.

1. **A:** Are you race fans?

   B: Not really, but we just won two tickets to the races in a grocery store contest.

   A: What _____*had*_____ you _____*been planning*_____ to do this weekend before you won your tickets?
   a. (plan)

   B: Go to the beach.

2. **A:** I'm speaking to Mr. John Daley, the trainer of today's winner, Calico Cat. Mr. Daley, before Calico went into the homestretch today, _____ you _____ Calico to take first prize?
   a. (expect)

   B: _____ In fact, I don't think anyone had. Calico wasn't the favorite today, or even
   b.
   the second choice.

3. **A:** As you all know, Marianne Semmes was riding the ill-fated Hampton Roads today. Ms. Semmes, your horse had a terrible accident. How _____ he _____ before he fell?
   a. (behave)

   B: Just fine. He'd been running very well, but the track was slippery, and I guess he just took a bad step.

4. **A:** Carl Ray owns Omega, the expected winner. Carl, when I saw you this afternoon before the race you seemed very upset. _____ you _____ about Omega?
   a. (worry)

B: _____ He'd been acting very fidgety before the race.
     b.

5. **A:** What brings you to the track today?

   B: My daughter. She's crazy about horses. For a long time, we weren't sure about coming.

     Today we finally decided to.

   A: Why _____ you _____ ?
                      a. (hesitate)

   B: It just seemed like a long trip to watch some horses run a mile and a half.

6. **A:** And here's Paul Boucher, one of the most experienced people here today. Paul, you retired

     last year. _____ you _____ it for a long time?
                             a. (consider)

   B: _____ For at least a year.
     b.

7. **A:** Now I'm standing in the clubhouse with Ken David, jockey for today's winner. Well, Ken,

     you and Calico surprised everyone here today. _____ you _____ a
                                           a. (anticipate)

     spectacular finish like that?

   B: _____ Not at all. No one was more surprised than I was this afternoon.
     b.

3. Affirmative and Negative Statements

*Look at these facts about Julie Krone's career. Then combine the phrases, using
the past perfect progressive to express the activity that occurred first. Use
negative forms when necessary.*

From the 1950s on		Judi, Julie's mother, trained horses for horse shows
1963		Julie Krone was born
1965	2 years old	Julie started riding horses
1967	4 years old	Judi started giving Julie lessons for competing in horse shows
1968	5 years old	Julie won first prize for riding at a state fair
1978	14 years old	decided to become a jockey
1979	15 years old	got her first job, as a groom at Churchill Downs, home of the Kentucky Derby
1980	16 years old	dropped out of high school and moved to Florida to live with her grandparents
Jan. 30, 1981	17 years old	rode her first race as a professional jockey
	5 weeks later	won her first race as a professional jockey
1982	19 years old	won riding title for best jockey in Atlantic City, N.J.
mid 1980s	in her 20s	started earning half a million dollars a year
1991–1992	27 and 28 years old	became first woman to enter the Belmont Stakes; lost both races
1993	29 years old	became the first woman to win the Belmont Stakes

(continued on next page)

1. Julie/be born

   her mother/train horses for many years

   When *Julie was born, her mother had been training horses for many years.*

2. Julie/turn three years old

   she/already/ride for a year

   By the time _____

3. her mother/only/teach her for a year

   Julie/win first prize in a state fair

   _____ before _____

4. Julie/think about becoming a jockey for very long

   she/get/her first job as a professional

   _____ when _____

5. she/enter her first race as a professional

   Julie/live with her parents for several months

   When _____

6. she/race for even two months

   she/win her first professional race

   _____ before _____

7. she/complete her first year as a professional

   she/attend high school for more than a year

   By the time _____

8. Julie/compete professionally for less than two years

   she/win a prize for best jockey at a famous track

   _____ when _____

9. she/earn half a million dollars a year

   she/win at Belmont

   _____ by the time _____

10. she/win first prize there

    Julie/lose at Belmont for two years

    Before _____

U N I T

4

**Future
Progressive**

1. Affirmative and Negative Statements

Complete this article with the future progressive form of the verbs in parentheses. Choose affirmative or negative.

An **old Approach to a new Problem**

Next year, Jayme and Bob Wilson _____*will be moving*_____ from
1. (move)

their rented two-bedroom city apartment to a place called Glenn

Commons. There they _____ in one of a row of houses
2. (live)

facing other houses, all conspicuously lacking fences, hedges, or other

barriers. They _____ in an area in back of the houses.
3. (park)

And even though there is a nice kitchen with a large window facing the

front of the house, the Wilsons _____ dinners there.
4. (prepare)

Jayme, Bob, and their two children _____ most
5. (eat)

evening meals along with twenty other families in a common house.

And they _____ there. Their house will be just a
6. (drive)

two-minute walk from the common area—a walk that will take them

along paths and greenery.

This doesn't sound like the suburbs. What's going on? The

Wilsons, along with a growing number of other people,

_____ to one of the many planned communities that
7. (relocate)

are beginning to spring up across the country. Called "co-housing,"

(continued on next page)

these communities feature cooperative living arrangements designed to counter some of the isolation and loneliness of suburban life.

While the Wilsons get to know their neighbors, they _____ also _____ money. For starters, they _____ a lawn mower or a
8. (save)   9. (buy)
washer-dryer since the community shares large equipment. And they _____
10. (pay)
food, utility, or child care bills as individuals either. Child care? Yes. The Wilsons

_____ anymore about what to do if one of their children has a cold and each
11. (worry)
parent is due at a business meeting in an hour. The center _____ for that.
12. (provide)

The Wilsons will, however, have some added responsibilities. For one thing, they will have to be much more involved in the development and operation of their community. Even before they move in, they _____ monthly meetings to determine how the
13. (attend)
community is run. And several times a month they'll be among the people preparing the dinners and providing the child care for the others. It's clearly not a lifestyle that will appeal to everyone.

Who started this new idea? Actually, the concept is quite old, tracing its roots to nineteenth-century European villages. It has been used in Denmark since 1972. Even though only a few co-housing communities have been completed in this country, we _____
14. (see)
more and more of them in the near future as people try to improve the quality of their lives by returning to some of the values of the past.

2. Questions and Short Answers

Use the future progressive or short answers to complete these conversations that take place at a co-housing meeting. Use negative forms when necessary.

1. (when/we/plant the garden?)

   A: *When will we be planting the garden?*

   B: Jack's bought the seed, so we should be ready to start this week.

2. Speaking of gardening, Martha, (you/use the lawn mower tomorrow?)

   A: _____

   B: _____ You can have it if you'd like.

3. You know, with more families moving in, the laundry facilities aren't adequate anymore.

   (when/we/get new washers?)

   A: _____

   B: The housing committee is getting information on brands and prices. They'll be ready to report

   on them at the next meeting.

4. Jack, (you/go to the post office/tomorrow?)

   A: _____

   B: _____ Can I mail something for you?

5. Janice, you and Ed are in charge of dinner Friday night. (what/you/make?)

   A: _____ Have you decided yet?

   B: How does vegetable soup, roast chicken, corn bread, salad, and chocolate chip cookies sound?

6. (who/watch the kids tomorrow?)

   A: _____ Al was supposed to do it, but he's still sick.

   B: That's no problem. I can take care of them.

7. (the entertainment committee/plan anything else in the near future?)

   A: _____ I really enjoyed that slide show last month.

   B: _____ We're thinking of organizing a Saturday night square dance.

8. As you know, this is my husband's and my first meeting. (we/meet every month?)

    A: _____

    B: _____ Meetings take place the fifteenth of every month.

9. I was just looking at my calendar. The fifteenth of next month is a Sunday. (we/still meet then?)

    A: _____

    B: _____ When the fifteenth falls on a weekend, we switch it to the

following Monday.

3. Future Progressive or Simple Present Tense

Look at Jayme and Bob Wilson's schedules for tomorrow. Complete the statements.

Jayme	
8:00	go to the post office
9:00	fax reports
10:00	have phone conference with John Smith
11:00	work on the Jansen report
12:00	lunch with Sara Neumann
1:00	bill clients
4:00	take Amanda to the dentist
5:00	shop for food
7:00	pay bills

Bob	
8:00	take the car in for inspection
9:00	meet with the boss
10:00	attend the time-management seminar
11:00	
12:00	lunch with Jack Allen
1:00	draft the A & W proposal
4:00	pick up the car
5:00	take Tommy to the barber
7:00	cut the grass

1. While Jayme _____ *goes to* _____ the post office, Bob
_____ *will be taking the car in for inspection* _____ .

2. Bob _____ his boss while Jayme

_____ .

3. While Bob _____ a time-management seminar, Jayme

_____ .

4. While Jayme _____ lunch with Sara Neumann, Bob

_____ .

5. Jayme _____ while Bob _____

_____ the A & W proposal.

6. While Bob _____ the car, Jayme

_____ .

7. Jayme _____ food while Bob

_____ .

8. While Jayme _____ the bills, Bob

_____ .

5

Future Perfect and Future Perfect Progressive ▼

1. Affirmative and Negative Statements

Complete the article with the future perfect or the future perfect progressive form of the verbs in parentheses.

As of December this year, Pam and Jessica Weiner

will have been working as personal time-management consultants
<u>   1. (work)</u>

for five years. Fed up with disorganization at home, Pam and Jessica

developed a system that worked so well that they started teaching

it to others. By this anniversary celebration, hundreds of people

_____ the Weiners' seminars, and these efficient
2. (complete)

sisters _____ them cope with chaos in their
3. (help)

personal lives.

    "What a difference their seminars made!" exclaimed Corinne

Smith, who completed the course a few years ago. "This December, I

_____ their system for two years. I used to do my
4. (use)

holiday shopping on December 23. This year, I _____
5. (buy)

all my gifts by November 1. And I _____ them too."
6. (wrap)

    Why do we need a system? "Our lives are so complicated that

we can't remember it all," explained Pam Weiner. "A good example

is a new family in our seminar. They have two children, they both work,

but they have no system. By Monday, they _____
7. (not plan)

the week's menu, and they _____ on a driving
8. (not decide)

schedule for the week's activities. That means by Friday, they

_____ probably _____ for days
9. (argue)

about these things."

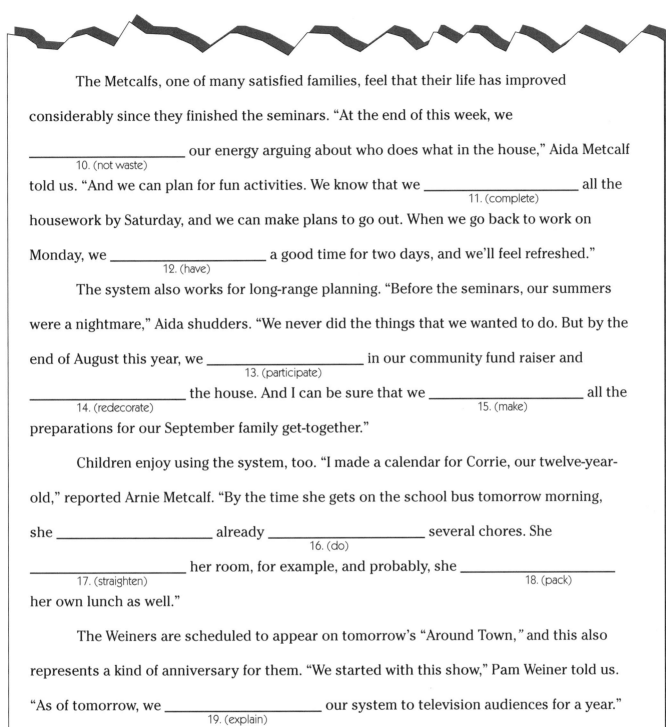

The Metcalfs, one of many satisfied families, feel that their life has improved considerably since they finished the seminars. "At the end of this week, we

_____ our energy arguing about who does what in the house," Aida Metcalf
10. (not waste)

told us. "And we can plan for fun activities. We know that we _____ all the
11. (complete)

housework by Saturday, and we can make plans to go out. When we go back to work on

Monday, we _____ a good time for two days, and we'll feel refreshed."
12. (have)

The system also works for long-range planning. "Before the seminars, our summers

were a nightmare," Aida shudders. "We never did the things that we wanted to do. But by the

end of August this year, we _____ in our community fund raiser and
13. (participate)

_____ the house. And I can be sure that we _____ all the
14. (redecorate)   15. (make)

preparations for our September family get-together."

Children enjoy using the system, too. "I made a calendar for Corrie, our twelve-year-

old," reported Arnie Metcalf. "By the time she gets on the school bus tomorrow morning,

she _____ already _____ several chores. She
16. (do)

_____ her room, for example, and probably, she _____
17. (straighten)   18. (pack)

her own lunch as well."

The Weiners are scheduled to appear on tomorrow's "Around Town," and this also

represents a kind of anniversary for them. "We started with this show," Pam Weiner told us.

"As of tomorrow, we _____ our system to television audiences for a year."
19. (explain)

2. Questions and Responses

Complete the conversations with short answers or the present perfect or present perfect progressive form of the verbs in parentheses.

1. **A:** I'm going shopping. 'Bye.

   B: I have to leave at two o'clock for a dentist appointment. _____*Will*_____ you

   _____*have brought*_____ the car back by then?
   <u>(bring)</u>

   A: _____ I don't have much to buy.

2. **A:** Corrie, your group is singing at the fund raiser next weekend, right? By three o'clock, how long

   _____ you _____ ?
   <u>(sing)</u>

   B: About half an hour. Why?

   A: There's a rock band from the high school that wants to start at three.

3. **A:** This is Aida. I'm in charge of the handicrafts booth this year. How many of those nice dish towels

   _____ you _____ by Sunday? Do you know?
   <u>(sew)</u>

   B: Oh, at least twenty.

4. **A:** Oh, no. I forgot about carpooling today.

   B: Suppose you leave right now. How long _____ the kids

   _____ by the time you get there?
   <u>(wait)</u>

   A: Only about fifteen minutes. I guess that's not a big deal.

5. **A:** Arnie, _____ the paint _____
   <u>(dry)</u>

   downstairs by the fifteenth?

   B: _____ We'd better give it until the sixteenth. Why?

   A: I want to hang the curtains.

6. **A:** _____ the cleaner _____ them by then?
   <u>(deliver)</u>

   B: _____ They promised me I'd have them on the twelfth.

7. **A:** Do you realize that September first is an anniversary? That's the date we moved into this house.

   B: How many years _____ we _____ here?
   <u>(live)</u>

   A: Ten. Amazing, isn't it?

3. Questions and Affirmative Statements

Look at the Metcalfs' calendar through September 4. Write questions and answers about their activities.

Sunday	Monday	Tuesday	Wednesday	Thursday	Friday	Saturday
1 Aida walk 1/2 mi every day	**2** Arnie paint first bedroom	**3** Arnie paint second bedroom	**4** Arnie paint bathroom	**5** Aida start driving in carpool for day camp	**6**	**7**
8 Aida water garden daily	**9** Start picking vegetables daily	**10**	**11** Arnie paint downstairs	**12**	**13**	**14**
15 Arnie finish painting indoors	**16** Arnie 4:00 p.m. dentist appointment	**17** Corrie pick blueberries for pies (need 3 quarts)	**18**	**19** Aida start baking pies for bake sale (agreed to bring 6 pies)	**20**	**21** Bake sale for fund raiser at Community Center
22 Aida start unpacking fall clothing	**23**	**24**	**25** Iron and put away fall clothing	**26** Last day of carpool	**27**	**28**
29 Aida and Arnie pack for trip to Mom and Dad's	**30**	**31** Travel to Mom and Dad's	**1**	**2** Arrive at 4:00 p.m.	**3**	**4** Annual family picnic

1. (how many miles/Aida/walk/by August 31?)

A: _____ *How many miles will Aida have walked by August 31?* _____

B: _____ *She'll have walked 15 1/2 miles.* _____

2. (how long/Aida/walk/by August 31?)

A: _____

B: _____

3. (how many rooms/Arnie/paint/by August 5?)

A: _____

B: _____

(continued on next page)

4. (how long/Arnie/paint/by August 15?)

   A: _____

   B: _____

5. (on August 16/Arnie/leave/for his dentist appointment/by four o'clock?)

   A: _____

   B: _____

6. (Aida/unpack/all the fall clothing/by August 23?)

   A: _____

   B: _____

7. (how long/Aida/drive in the carpool/by August 19?)

   A: _____

   B: _____

8. (how many quarts of blueberries/Corrie/pick/by August 19?)

   A: _____

   B: _____

9. (how many pies/Aida and Corrie/bake/by August 21?)

   A: _____

   B: _____

10. (they/finish/packing for the trip/by August 31?)

    A: _____

    B: _____

11. (how long/family/travel/when they arrive at Mom and Dad's?)

    A: _____

    B: _____

12. (they/have/their picnic/by September 3?)

    A: _____

    B: _____

1. Affirmative and Negative Tag Questions and Short Answers

A couple wants to rent an apartment. Complete their questions to the landlord. Provide short answers based on the apartment ad.

> **N. Smithfield unfurn. 1 BR in owner occup. bldg., renovated kitchen w. all new appliances, incl. DW, near all transp. & shopping, $500/mo. + util., avail. for immed. occup. No pets. 272-7738**

1. **A:** The rent is $500, *isn't it?* _____

   B: _____ *Yes, it is.* _____

2. **A:** It includes electricity, _____

   B: _____

3. **A:** It isn't furnished, _____

   B: _____

4. **A:** You've renovated the kitchen, _____

   B: _____

5. **A:** The kitchen doesn't have a dishwasher, _____

   B: _____

6. **A:** You just put in a new refrigerator, _____

   B: _____

7. **A:** There's a bus nearby, _____

   B: _____

8. **A:** I can't move in right away, _____

   B: _____

9. **A:** You won't allow pets, _____

   B: _____

10. **A:** You live right in the building, _____

    B: _____

2. Affirmative and Negative Tag Questions

Complete these conversations with question tags and the correct form of the verbs in parentheses.

1. **A:** You _____*moved*_____ in last week, didn't you?
   a. (move)

   B: Yes. You haven't been living here very long yourself, _____*have you*_____?
   b.

   A: Oh, it's been about a year now.

   B: It _____ a nice place to live, isn't it?
   c. (be)

   A: We think so.

2. **A:** You _____ the letter carrier this morning, have you?
   a. (see)

   B: No, why?

   A: I don't think our mail is being forwarded from our old address.

   B: You filled out one of those change-of-address forms, _____?
   b.

   A: Yes. But that was almost a month ago. Our mail should be coming here

   by now, _____?
   c.

   B: I would think so.

3. **A:** There's an all-night supermarket nearby, _____?
   a.

   B: Yes. It's on 10th and Walnut.

   A: Oh. I know where that is. There used to be a restaurant there, _____?
   b.

   B: That's right. They closed down last year.

   A: That's strange. They _____ there very long, had they?
   c. (be)

   B: Just about a year. The location just wasn't good for a restaurant.

4. **A:** The new neighbors are really friendly, _____?
   a.

   B: Yes. That reminds me. The people across the hall invited us over for coffee and cake on

   Saturday. You haven't made any plans for then, _____?
   b.

   A: Well, I was going to work on our taxes.

   B: You _____ a little break, can't you?
   c. (take)

   A: Sure. Why not?

3. Affirmative and Negative Tag Questions

The new tenants are going to visit their neighbors. They want to confirm some of the assumptions they have. Rewrite their ideas, using tag questions.

1. We think the people in apartment 4F have lived here a long time.

   The people in apartment 4F have lived here a long time, haven't they?

2. I don't think our apartment had been occupied for a while.

   Our apartment hadn't been occupied for a while, had it?

3. We believe this is a good building.

   _____

4. It seems that the owner takes good care of it.

   _____

5. It looks like he recently redid the lobby.

   _____

6. I have the impression he doesn't talk very much.

   _____

7. I don't think the rent will increase next year.

   _____

8. I don't believe that all the apartments are occupied.

   _____

9. It looks like some new people will be moving into apartment 1B.

   _____

10. We have the impression that this is really a nice place to live.

   _____

U N I T

7

Additions and
Responses
with *So, Too,
Neither, Not
either, and
But*

1. **Affirmative or Negative**

Complete the additions and responses in the following article. Choose between affirmative and negative forms.

Helen Diller has a lot in common with her neighbor Susan Brown. Helen works full time, and _____*so*_____ does Susan.
1.
Helen has just hired a sitter for her baby. Susan _____
2.
too. And they're both careful parents. Helen interviewed a lot of people before deciding on the best person for the job. So _____
3.
Susan.

There's one crucial difference, however. Helen's Brendan is a human baby, _____ Susan's Agnes isn't. Agnes is a
4.
Great Dane, a thoroughbred dog the size of a small pony.

Susan says, "I feel very responsible for Agnes. It's like having a child. Helen can't leave her baby alone for ten hours every day, and _____ can I. Both Brendan and Agnes need human
5.
contact and care during the day."

Jack Austin, owner of PetCare, agrees. "Human children are sociable creatures, and so _____ pets, especially dogs.
6.
Isolation is painful for them and bad for their health too."

"Most of us think of our pets as our babies," continued Austin. "My friends who are parents don't mind buying the best food for their babies, and I don't _____. They want their kids to go
7.
to the best schools, and so _____ I."
8.
Schools? Are we carrying this comparison a little too far? "Not at all," Austin assured us. "Our puppy kindergarten performs the same service for dogs as a human kindergarten does for children. A five-year-old city child will need to learn about his or her environment, and so _____ a puppy. A child will need to develop social
9.
skills, and a puppy will _____." Austin's company
10.
even offers play dates so that shy dogs can make new friends.

"A lot of my friends think I'm extravagant," laughed Susan, "but I _____. I have my social contacts, and _____
11.   12.
does Agnes. The peace of mind is worth the expense."

2.   Affirmative or Negative

Complete the conversation with additions and responses. Choose betweeen affirmative and negative forms.

A: How did you and Roger meet?

B: Well, I own a dog, and _____*so*_____ _____*does*_____ Roger. My dog, Agnes, and I used
                                                            1.

to walk in the park every morning, and Roger and Booboo _____ _____.
                                                                                    2.

A: So you got to know each other walking your dogs?

B: Yep. Agnes doesn't like her leash, and _____ _____ Booboo. One
                                                                    3.

morning they were both walking off the leash. Agnes started chasing a squirrel, and

_____ _____ Booboo.
                4.

A: The same squirrel?

B: Right. Roger caught Booboo, but I couldn't catch Agnes. And Roger

_____ _____. She's huge, you know. She ran right out of sight.
                5.

A: What did you do?

B: Well, I wanted to give up and call the police, _____ Roger _____.
                                                                            6.

He kept on looking for her while I held Booboo.

A: So you invited him to dinner and found out that you had a lot in common.

B: Right. I'm crazy about dogs, and _____ _____ Roger. In fact,
                                                        7.

I've never been without one, and he _____ _____.
                                                    8.

A: Don't you two disagree about anything?

B: Sure. Lots of things. He wants to move out of the city, _____ I _____.
                                                                                    9.`

I love it here.

3. Affirmative or Negative

Look at the requirements of various pets. Then complete the sentences below with appropriate additions and responses about the pets named in parentheses.

Choosing the Right Pet

	Dogs	Cats	Birds	Fish
Housing	need bed	need bed	need cage	need aquarium
Food	once a day	twice a day	food always available	once or twice a day; remove uneaten food
Care and Grooming	more than 1 hour a day; need grooming	1/2 hour a day; need grooming	1/2 hour a day; no grooming	1 hour a week; no grooming
Company and Attention Your Pet Needs from You	a lot	a medium amount	a medium amount	none
Life Span	10 years or more	10 years or more	canaries: 5-10 years parrots: 60 years or more	2-10 years
Veterinary Care	yearly visits	yearly visits	when sick	when sick
Expense	medium	medium	low	low

1. Dogs need their own bed, _____*and so do cats*_____.
   (cats)

2. Birds should have food available at all times, _____.
   (fish)

3. Cats must have specific mealtimes, _____.
   (dogs)

4. Birds don't require a lot of time for care, _____.
   (fish)

5. Dogs and cats need grooming, _____.
   (birds and fish)

6. A dog needs a lot of companionship, _____.
   (a fish)

7. A bird can get along without much attention, _____.
   (a fish)

8. Dogs and cats will live at least ten years, _____.
   (some fish)

9. Parrots have a life span of more than 60 years, _____.
   (other pets)

10. Birds don't need to see the vet regularly, _____.
    (fish)

11. Dogs have to get a checkup every year, _____.
    (cats)

12. Fish don't cost much to keep, _____.
    (birds)

1. Gerund or Infinitive

Complete this news report with the correct form of the verbs in parentheses. Choose between gerunds and infinitives.

AMA POLICYMAKERS WANT

ENTERTAINMENT INDUSTRY

to Change **RATING**
1. (change)

SYSTEMS

The American Medical Association wants the entertainment

industry _____ more
2. (provide)

descriptive ratings on all kinds of entertainment—from movies to

music recordings. _____
3. (overhaul)

the entire rating system was strongly

suggested by the AMA at their

annual meeting last week.

The powerful, 300,000-

member AMA will now try

_____ the industry
4. (convince)

_____ its recommenda-
5. (adopt)

tions. This may not be easy

_____ since industry
6. (do)

spokespeople cry censorship at

attempts _____ violence
7. (curb)

on big and small screens. However,

_____ programs is not
8. (censor)

the AMA's intention, states Robert

E. McAfee, the AMA's new president.

McAfee says physicians simply

want _____ parents
9. (help)

_____ their jobs more
10. (perform)

effectively. Since violent programming

comes into everyone's home, and

any four- or five-year-old can witness

it, ". . . we have every right as

physicians _____ to do
11. (begin)

prevention," claimed McAfee.

The AMA bases its recom-

mendations on studies which show

that children seem _____
12. (learn)

aggressive habits early in life. As

adults, they resist _____
13. (change)

these habits. The harmful conse-

quences may last a lifetime.

In its reply to the AMA

recommendations, NBC did not offer

_____ its practices. A
14. (alter)

spokesperson said that the network

(continued on next page)

had long ago started _____
15. (regulate)

its own shows. Furthermore, NBC has already

advised parents _____ certain
16. (not turn on)

programs during family viewing times because

they are unsuitable for children. The other

networks apparently decided _____
17. (not respond)

to requests for comment.

It's also necessary _____ the
18. (update)

movie rating system, says the AMA. Current

ratings divide children into three age groups—

up to twelve years, thirteen to sixteen, and

seventeen or older. However, these ratings fail

_____ into account important
19. (take)

mental and emotional stages in children. The

AMA wants ratings _____
20. (use)

separate categories for ages three to seven,

eight to twelve, and thirteen to seventeen. "Any

parent who remembers _____ an
21. (take)

easily scared seven-year-old to a movie

rated PG-13 will probably agree with this

recommendation," commented one doctor.

_____ the movie rating
22. (redo)

system is not a task that creates enthusiasm at

the Motion Picture Association. Spokesperson

Barbara Dixon said that the MPA is always

willing _____ to criticism about its
23. (listen)

rating system. However, she added, "We're

hesitant _____ something that's
24. (change)

worked so well."

Many feel it is unrealistic

_____ more responsible attitudes
25. (expect)

by the industry. However, makers of com-

puter and video games are taking steps

_____ their products. The Software
26. (rate)

Publishers Association is planning a rating

system that they will use _____
27. (warn)

consumers of violent content in new game

packages. However, the system will not require

a retailer to stop _____ violent
28. (sell)

games to children.

Homicides have grown six times

faster than the population in the United States.

In the face of statistics like these, Congress

will soon force the entertainment industry

_____ some initiative for social
29. (take)

change. Under the circumstances, the industry

is likely _____ tighter regulation
30. (face)

in the near future. Many feel that the industry

might as well volunteer _____
31. (impose)

controls of its own as soon as possible.

Source: Brenda C. Coleman, The Associated Press, June 15, 1994.

2. Gerund or Infinitive

Complete this interview with a doctor about the AMA report. Use the words in the box and the correct form of the verbs in parentheses. Choose between gerunds and infinitives.

~~shocked~~	likely	fed up with	used to	unwilling

A: I was _____*shocked*_____ _____*to read*_____ that children will see 40,000 acts of violence
1. (read)

on television before they grow up. I had no idea it was that bad.

B: Yes, that is an alarming statistic.

A: It also appears that the networks are _____ _____. They seem
2. (change)

pretty satisfied with things the way they are.

B: Yes, I think that they're _____ _____ all the responsibility on
3. (put)

the viewer. That's the way it's always been, and they're accustomed to it.

A: The networks may not want to change, but I know a lot of us are

_____ _____ violence during family viewing times. We're really
4. (see)

sick of it. A lot of my friends don't even turn on the cartoons anymore.

B: That's probably a good idea. Several studies show that all children are more

_____ _____ others after they watch violent cartoons.
5. (hit)

It's really quite predictable.

decide	dislike	hesitate	stop	force

A: OK. Now what can we do about this problem?

B: Well, viewers can make a big differencce. First of all, we have to put a lot of pressure on the

networks and _____ them _____ shows for violence. They'll
6. (rate)

give in if enough viewers tell them they must.

(continued on next page)

A: What else?

B: When you see something you don't like, pick up the phone immediately. Don't wait.

We shouldn't _____ _____ the networks about material that we
$\qquad$ 7. (tell)

find offensive. Recently a network _____ _____ a violent ad for
$\qquad$ 8. (run)

another show right in the middle of a family sitcom. So many people complained that they

reversed that decision and _____ _____ the ad in that time slot.
$\qquad$ 9. (show)

A: Violence bothers my kids, but they _____ _____ a show once
$\qquad$ 10. (turn off)

it starts. They want to stick it out to the end.

dream of   forbid   permit   insist on

B: This is where parents have to assert their authority and _____ _____ the
$\qquad$ 11. (change)

channel when violence appears. Sometimes they'll face a lot of resistance, but they should be firm.

A: You know, in a lot of families, parents work until six. They can't successfully

_____ _____ certain shows. They're just not around to
$\qquad$ 12. (turn on)

enforce the rules.

B: Help is coming from the electronics industry in the form of a V-chip.

A: What exactly is a V-chip?

B: It's a chip that will be built into television sets. The V-chip won't

_____ _____ violent shows. It blocks them electronically.
$\qquad$ 13. (tune in)

A: It sounds like something all parents _____ _____.
$\qquad$ 14. (own)

3.   Objects with Gerunds and Infinitives

Read the conversations about watching television. Then write summary statements.

1. **Kids:** Can we watch "Biker Mice from Mars," Mom? Please? Just this once?

   Mom: I'm sorry, but it's just too violent. How about "Beakman's World"?

   Summary: _____ *The mother didn't allow them to watch it.* _____
                                       (the mother / allow / they / watch it)

2. **Annie:** Our parents just bought a V-chip.

   Bea: What's that?

   Annie: It's something that blocks violent shows so we can't watch them on our TV.

   Summary: _____
                               (a V-chip / interfere with / they / watch / violent shows)

3. **Roger:** Beakman really wants viewers to send in science questions.

   Cora: I know. He keeps on telling them that their questions are great.

   Summary: _____
                               (Beakman / encourage / they / send in questions)

4. **Dad:** You were having some pretty bad nightmares last night, Jennifer. I think you'd better stop

   watching those cop shows.

   Jennifer: OK, but I really love them.

   Summary: _____
                               (the father / object to / Jennifer / watch / cop shows)

5. **Students:** We want to watch the TV news, but the reporting on adult news shows is

   really frightening.

   Teacher: Try "Nick News." It won an award for news reporting for kids.

   Summary: _____
                               (the teacher / recommend / they / watch / "Nick News")

6. **Sue:** I'll never forget that great Knicks game we watched last year.

   Bob: What Knicks game?

   Sue: Don't you remember? We saw it together! The Knicks beat the Rockets, 91–85.

   Summary: _____
                               (Bob / remember / they / see / that game)

7. **Fred:** Does Sharif still watch "Z-Men" every Saturday?

   Abu: No. We explained that it was too violent for him, and he decided not to watch it anymore.

   Summary: _____
                               (Sharif's parents / persuade / he / watch "Z-Men")

8. **Mom:** Sara, it's nine o'clock. Time to turn off the TV.

   Sara: Oh, Mom. Just a little longer, OK?

   Mom: You know the rules. No TV after nine o'clock.

   Summary: _____

   (the mother / insist on / Sara / turn off the TV)

9. **Aziza:** This is boring. What's on the other channels?

   Ben: I don't know. Where's the remote control?

   Summary: _____

   (Aziza / want / Ben / change the channel)

10. **Nick:** Wow! This is great!

   Paul: How can you watch this stuff? It's so violent.

   Summary: _____

   (Paul / can't understand / Nick / watch / the show)

1. Differentiating Meaning: *Make, Have, Let, Help, Get*

Complete this article about math teacher Jaime Escalante by circling the correct verb.

Born in Bolivia, Jaime Escalante emigrated to the United States to follow his passion—teaching mathematics. He did this at Garfield High, an East Los Angeles high school noted for its tough students and high drop-out rate of almost 55 percent. The school administration was so ineffective that they (let)/made gangs of students (and nonstudents) roam the halls and spray the walls with graffiti. Escalante changed all that. A strict disciplinarian, he let/made students do massive amounts of homework, take daily quizzes, and fill out daily time cards. He believed in his students' ability to succeed and would never get/let them drop out of class. He considered vacations a waste of time and let/made his students do homework during the semester break. He even planned two full mornings of classes during spring vacation. He wasn't going to let/make a school vacation erase what his students had learned!

Escalante often used nontraditional methods. To develop a spirit of camaraderie, he got/had his students to do football-like cheers before the start of class. He praised them, teased them,

(continued on next page)

Verbs
Followed
by Objects and
the Base Form:
*Make, Have,
Let, Help*

insulted them—anything that worked. Most of all, he <u>got/helped</u> them believe in
7.

themselves. Then he did the impossible. He <u>had/let</u> them take the Advanced
8.

Placement exam, a national test that only 2 percent of high school students take. This

difficult exam, consisting mostly of calculus, gives students college credit for high school

work. In preparation for the test, Escalante <u>let/made</u> his class work harder than
9.

ever. Because the results on the tests were so high, and because many students made the

same kind of error in one of the problems, the company that published the test suspected

his students of cheating. To prove their innocence, Escalante decided to <u>get/have</u> them
10.

take the test again. To ensure that no cheating could occur, the official administering the

test <u>let/made</u> them sit at desks spaced wide apart. Everyone passed, proving
11.

once and for all that even students from "disadvantaged" backgrounds could succeed.

Escalante's story became well known when film director Ramón Menéndez

made the movie *Stand and Deliver*. Escalante <u>got/let</u> the actor Edward James Olmos,
12.

who plays him in the film, spend eighteen hours a day with him. Escalante, as well as

movie critics and theater critics, were pleased with the results.

What makes Escalante such an effective teacher? In the words of one of his

students, Escalante "really cares. He <u>let/made</u> us feel powerful, that we could
13.

do anything."

2. Affirmative and Negative Statements

At the beginning of the semester, Jaime Escalante handed out a list of instructions similar to this.

SUBJECT GRADE

Tests		Quizzes
A	90–100%	7
B	80–89%	6
C	70–79%	5
D	60–69%	4

TESTS (100 points each): All tests will be on *Fridays* and you must take them in class. *No make-up* tests will be given.

QUIZZES (10 points each): Almost every day and must be taken in class; *no make-up* quizzes will be given.

HOMEWORK (10 points each): All homework assignments will be collected. When turned in the paper should have your name, period, and homeroom number. They must be written in the upper-right corner.

WORK HABITS: No late homework or make-up work will be accepted.

COOPERATION: Five tardies* = U

NOTEBOOK (possible 50 points): Each student will keep a notebook, not a pee-chee folder or any other type of loose file, in which he/she shall keep his/her work composed of two sections:
  i. Class notes (you should take notes carefully in class)
  ii. Quizzes and tests
  On Fridays each student shall submit his/her notebook to the teacher for credit.

ATTENDANCE: You are expected to attend the class daily. If you are absent five (5) times during the semester, you will be referred to the Dean. If you miss three (3) tests during the semester, you may be referred to your counselor.

PLACE THIS PAPER IN YOUR NOTEBOOK
FOR A BETTER EDUCATION

_____   _____
Student's Signature   J.A. Escalante
                                   Mathematics Teacher

* *tardies* = latenesses

Use the information above to complete these sentences about Escalante's class.

1. He _____*made them take*_____ tests every Friday.
   (make / take)

2. He _____ make-up tests.
   (let / take)

3. He _____ quiz questions almost every day.
   (have / answer)

4. He _____ their homework assignments.
   (make / hand in)

5. He _____ their homework late.
   (let / submit)

6. He _____ their names in the upper right corner.
   (have / write)

7. He _____ late four times before giving them a grade of U.
   (let / come)

8. He _____ their notebooks every week.
   (have / submit)

9. He _____ the sheet.
   (make / sign)

10. He _____ a neatly organized notebook.
    (have / keep)

11. He _____ to the dean if they missed three tests.
    (make / go)

12. The purpose of these rules was to _____ well in the course.
    (help / do)

3. Affirmative and Negative Statements

Read these short conversations, which take place in Mrs. Olinski's math class.
Complete the summary sentences, using the verbs in parentheses.

1. **Marta:** Can we please take a short break?

   Mrs. O.: Sure. We'll break for ten minutes.

   Summary: The teacher _____*let them take a break*_____.
   (let)

2. **Mark:** I can't solve this problem. Can you show me how to do it?

   Mrs. O.: It's better if you work it out yourself.

   Summary: She _____.
   (make)

3. **Don:** I'm having trouble keeping up with the rest of the class.

   Mrs. O.: My doors are open all day. Students can come by anytime for help.

   Summary: She always _____.
   (let)

4. **Sara:** The answer is 5.34.

   Mrs. O.: No. I'll give you one more chance to get it right. Try again.

   Summary: She _____.
   (make)

5. **Mrs. O.:** Your homework is a mess. I'd like you to do it over.

Robert: Oh, OK.

Summary: She _____.
(have)

6. **Delia:** Can we use our calculators during the trigonometry exam?

Mrs. O.: Absolutely not.

Summary: She _____.
(let)

7. **Mrs. O.:** I would really appreciate it if some of you would help clean up this classroom.

David: OK. We'll do it.

Summary: She _____.
(get)

8. **Mrs. O.:** You got the right answer. Now describe the process to me.

Ken: OK.

Summary: She _____.
(have)

10

The Passive: Overview

▼

PART V: PASSIVE

1. Active and Passive

*Complete the chart. Use **they** in active sentences when you don't know the subject.*

ACTIVE	PASSIVE
1. They print the paper daily.	*The paper is printed daily*.
2. *They discovered the mistake in time*.	The mistake was discovered in time.
3. They fired Alice and Jay.	_____.
4. They delivered the copies yesterday.	_____.
5. _____.	The article was written by Al Baker.
6. _____.	New editors are frequently hired.
7. Marla Jacobson interviewed the new editor.	_____.
8. _____.	Marla was given an assignment on the Philippines.

2. Passive Statements: Simple Present and Simple Past Tenses

Complete these facts about the Philippines. Use the appropriate passive form of the verbs in parentheses.

1. The Philippines _____*were named*_____ by the Spanish
   (name)
   explorer Villalobos in 1534.

2. The islands _____ Felipinas to honor the
   (call)
   prince of Asturias, who later became the king of Spain.

3. Today, the country _____ officially as the
   (know)
   Republic of the Philippines.

4. The Philippines _____ of 7,100 islands.
   (make up)

5. Only eleven of them _____ major islands.
   (consider)

6. An old legend says that the Philippines _____
   (form)
   when a giant threw a huge mass of rock into the sea.

7. Many of the tiny islands _____ names.
   (not give)

8. The two largest islands _____ Mindanao and Luzon.
   (call)

3. Active or Passive

Here are some more facts about the Philippines. Choose between the active and passive form of the verbs in parentheses.

1. The Philippines _____ *are located* _____ in the tropics.
   (locate)

2. Most people _____ *live* _____ in the lowlands.
   (live)

3. Even the mountains _____.
   (inhabit)

4. Large rivers _____ on the main islands.
   (find)

5. Floods often _____ roads and bridges.
   (damage)

6. Windstorms _____ property damage and loss of life.
   (cause)

7. Long ago, most of the land _____ by forests.
   (cover)

8. Today, forests _____ over 70,000 square miles of the total area.
   (cover)

9. They _____ more than 3,000 kinds of trees.
   (contain)

10. Wild hogs _____ on most of the islands.
    (find)

11. Water buffalos _____ for cultivating the flooded rice fields.
    (use)

12. About 1,000 species of birds and 2,000 species of fish _____ in
    (know)

    the Philippines.

4. The Passive: With or Without an Agent

Complete this information about the Philippines. Use the passive form of the verb in the first set of parentheses. Include the agent in the second set of parentheses only when necessary.

1. When the Spanish explorers came to the Philippines, the islands _____ *were inhabited* _____
   (inhabit)

   by three groups of people _____.
   (three groups of people)

2. The Aëtas _____ *are believed* _____ to be the earliest inhabitants.
   (believe)   (people)

3. Thousands of years later, the Aëta _____.
   (follow)   (groups from Indonesia)

4. Today, eight languages and almost ninety dialects _____
   (speak)   (the Filipinos)

   in the Philippines.

(continued on next page)

5. Since many of the dialects are similar, usually one dialect _____
(understand)

_____ .
(speakers of another dialect)

6. In 1937, Tagalog _____ to be
(declare)   (President Manuel Quezon)

the official language of the Philippines.

7. By 1970, Tagalog _____ .
(speak)   (55 percent of the Filipinos)

8. Today it _____ .
(speak)   (43 million people)

9. Tagalog belongs to the Austronesian language family, which _____

_____ all across the Pacific, from Hawaii to Taiwan.
(speak)   (people)

10. English _____ for commercial and business purposes.
(use)   (people)

5.   Questions and Short Answers

Look at the map of Bolivia.

✹	rubber
🐑	sheep
🐂	cattle
🦙	llamas
⚒	oil
G	gold
S	silver
T	tin
🌾	wheat
☺	potatoes
🌽	corn
🍇	fruits and nuts
🍃	tobacco
🪵	logging

Ask and answer questions. Use the passive.

1. tin/mine/in the north?

A: _____ *Is tin mined in the north?* _____

B: _____ *No, it isn't.* _____

2. What other minerals/mine?

A: _____

B: _____

3. Where/fruits and nuts/grow?

A: _____

B: _____

4. llamas/find/in the east?

A: _____

B: _____

5. Where/logging/do?

A: _____

B: _____

6. What animals/raise?

A: _____

B: _____

7. potatoes/grow?

A: _____

B: _____

8. Where/rubber/produce?

A: _____

B: _____

1. Active and Passive

*Complete the chart. Use **they** in active sentences when you don't know the subject.*

ACTIVE	PASSIVE
1. *Many countries should build new airports soon.*	New airports should be built by many countries soon.
2. They will construct some new airports on islands.	_____ _____
3. _____ _____	Passenger facilities might be put on decks under the runways.
4. They could save a lot of space that way.	_____ _____
5. _____ _____	A new airport will be built by Japan in Osaka Bay.
6. They have to create an artificial island for the airport.	_____ _____
7. _____ _____	Huge amounts of earth have got to be moved from nearby mountains.
8. Hong Kong will also build an island airport.	_____ _____
9. _____ _____	The island can't be reached right now except by boat.
10. _____ _____	Bridges and tunnels must be provided by airport planners.

2. Affirmative and Negative Statements

Complete this article with the passive form of the verbs in parentheses.
Choose between affirmative and negative forms.

While astronauts are working out cultural differences on the space station, people

here on earth ___*could be brought*___ closer together than ever before. Engineers believe
    1. (could / bring)

that all the continents _____ by bridges and tunnels. And these ventures
    2. (can / link)

_____ very soon. Many of the planned bridge and tunnel systems
    3. (may / launch)

_____ by the turn of the century. Here's a sample of places that
    4. (will / complete)

_____ by some of these projects:
    5. (be going to / connect)

England and Europe. The Chunnel between France and England, the first of these

projects, opened officially this week. When the tunnel begins full operation in the autumn,

freight and passengers _____ by trains under the English Channel.
    6. (will / carry)

Unfortunately for driving enthusiasts, motorists _____ to drive their cars
    7. (will / permit)

through the Chunnel. Instead, automobiles _____ by rail.
    8. (be going to / transport)

Asia and North America. In the next century, Asia and North America

_____ for the first time in 15,000 years. According to a Japanese planning
    9. (may / join)

group, small islands in the Bering Strait _____ by bridges carrying a
    10. (could / span)

railroad line.

Africa and Europe. The United Nations is now discussing a Gibraltar bridge,

but revolutionary techniques _____ for this project, since a bridge
    11. (have to / develop)

would be three times higher than any bridge ever built. A distance of at least

9.2 miles _____.
    12. (must / span)

Thailand, Malay Peninsula. The Trans-Thai Landbridge _____
    13. (will / build)

from the Andaman Sea to the Gulf of Thailand. New ports and towns _____
    14. (will / include)

in this project.

Italy and Sicily. Every year, 14 million people cross the Straits of Messina between

Sicily and Italy. The dream of completing a highway for them has been promised by the end of

(continued on next page)

this century, but it _____ by then. Frequent earthquakes and 125-m.p.h.
                            15. (might / fulfill)
winds in the area mean that some delays _____. These problems
                                              16. (can / avoid)
_____, promise engineers, who propose a two-mile extension bridge that can
        17. (will / solve)
withstand both quakes and high winds.

3. Questions and Short Answers

*Complete this interview with a Chunnel official, using the words in parentheses
or short answers.*

A: I'd like to ask some questions about the Chunnel, if you don't mind.

   First, _____*can*_____ cars _____*be driven*_____ through?
                                        1. (can / drive)

B: _____ Vehicles will be carried on a train called Le Shuttle.
              2.

A: _____ vehicles _____ by their drivers?
                                      3. (must / accompany)

B: _____ Motorists have to drive their cars onto the train and stay
              4.
   with them during the trip.

A: _____ drivers _____ to stay in their cars
                                    5. (will / require)
   during the trip?

B: _____ They can get out and walk alongside their cars if they like.
              6.

A: _____ food service _____?
                                          7. (be going to / provide)

B: _____ At this point, we can't offer food service. However, the ride
              8.
   is only about thirty-five minutes long.

A: _____ reservations _____ for Le Shuttle?
                                          9. (can / make)

B: _____ We're taking passengers only on a first-come, first-served
              10.
   basis. However, the Eurostar, which carries passengers through the Chunnel, is taking

   reservations now. Service will start in the summer.

A: I've heard that there might be some problems with Eurostar.

   _____ service _____ this summer?
                                  11. (could / delay)

B: _____ Coaches might not be delivered on time. But we're hoping for
              12.
   the best.

1. Passive Causatives

Complete the chart.

ACTIVE	PASSIVE CAUSATIVE
1. Someone does my taxes every April.	*I have my taxes done every April.*
2. Someone is painting my house.	
3. Someone checked my car last month.	
4. Someone has just cleaned our windows.	
5. Someone must do our repairs.	
6. Someone is going to fix our roof.	
7. Marie will cut my hair.	
8. Someone should check our electric wiring.	

2. Affirmative Statements

Complete this article about consumer fraud. Use the passive causative form of the verbs in parentheses.

Getting a $ Charge for Nothing

*I*n the aftermath of disasters such as the Los Angeles earthquake of 1994, consumers should be prepared to guard against fraud. Faced with structural damage to their homes, families must _____*get*_____ major repairs _____*done*_____. Working under great stress,
1. (get / do)

(continued on next page)

they sometimes _____ work _____ without obtaining

2. (have / complete)

estimates first. Often they _____ it _____ by dishonest

3. (have / do)

contractors because they haven't checked with the Better Business Bureau first. The following

is a case in point.

After the Los Angeles earthquake

in 1994, many people wanted to

_____ their electric wiring

systems _____. One

4. (get / test)

electrician told a woman that she had to

_____ her circuit breakers

_____ and charged her

5. (have / replace)

$510 per breaker. The same breakers cost

just $21.86 apiece in a hardware store.

"Dateline," a television news show on NBC,

decided to _____ the

story _____. Using a

6. (have / investigate)

hidden camera, they filmed the electrician's

visit to another customer. Like the customer

above, this customer _____

a new circuit breaker _____

7. (have / install)

to replace a broken one. But he was also

told that he should _____

five other ones _____

8. (get / replace)

for a charge of $356.00. Furthermore,

said the electrician, if the customer

_____ the job

_____ immediately,

9. (not have / do)

there was a risk of fire. "Dateline"

_____ the "broken" circuit

breakers _____. Not only

10. (have / test)

did they not need replacement, but the

electrician then went on to resell the "bad"

breakers to other unsuspecting customers.

Of course the majority of workers

are honest. But how can you, the consumer,

guard against those who aren't? Here are

some guidelines:

• Be a smart consumer.

Do business only with service

people you know are reputable. Before

retaining unknown professionals,

_____ them

_____ by appropriate

11. (have / check out)

agencies to see that they are properly

licensed. And although the Better Business

Bureau will not make recommendations,

they *will* tell you if they have received any complaints about a company.

• Use a credit card if you can.

This way, if there is any problem, you can _____ payment

_____ until the issue is
    12. (have / stop)

resolved. Your credit-card company will even help you try to resolve the conflict.

• Get an estimate.

Always try to get an estimate,

and _____ it

_____ in writing.
    13. (have / put)

• Know where to go for help.

If you think you have been a victim of fraud, notify the appropriate agency. Your state's Attorney General's Office is a good place to start. And don't forget the role of the media! In many cities, newspaper and TV reporters specialize in consumer advocacy. Even if you don't resolve the problem that way, you will at least have the satisfaction of _____ it

_____.
    14. (get / publicize)

---

3.   *Yes/No* and *Wh-* Questions

John is talking to his friend Frank about his car. Complete Frank's questions.
Use the passive causative.

1. **Frank:** My old Ford's been giving me trouble lately. (Where/usually/get/your car/service?)

    Where do you usually get your car serviced?

    John: I always go to Majestic Motors.

2. **Frank:** (How often/get/it/do?)

    _____

    John: Oh, about every 5,000 miles. In fact, I was there just yesterday.

3. **Frank:** Really? (get/it/winterize?)

    _____

    John: Well, he put antifreeze in the radiator.

4. **Frank:** (ever/get/snow tires/put on?)

    _____

John: No, I haven't. We really don't get enough snow around here for that. But we *are* going to

take a trip to Canada this winter.

5. **Frank:** (get/snow tires/put on/for the trip?)

_____

John: I guess it's not a bad idea.

6. **Frank:** You bought your car in 1993. Right? (How often/get/it/check/since then?)

_____

John: I can't say exactly. I do a lot of driving so I've brought it in a lot.

7. **Frank:** And you always have the work done at Majestic. (Why/get/it/do/there?)

_____

John: The guy who owns it is a good mechanic, and I trust him. I know he'd never rip me off.

4. Affirmative and Negative Statements

*John brought his car into Majestic Motors. Look at this portion of the checklist of services. Then write all the things John had or didn't have done. Use the causative with **have** or **get**.*

Majestic Motors

[✔] **check tire pressure**   [ ] **replace air filter**

[ ] **change oil**   [ ] **rotate tires**

[ ] **inspect undercarriage**   [ ] **adjust timing and engine speed**

[✔] **lubricate body and chassis**   [✔] **service automatic transmission**

[✔] **inspect air filter**   [✔] **flush cooling system**

1. _____ *He had the tire pressure checked.* _____

2. _____

3. _____

4. _____

5. _____

6. _____

7. _____

8. _____

9. _____

10. _____

Answer Key

Note: In this answer key, where the contracted form is given, the full form is also correct, and where the full form is given, the contracted form is also correct.

PART I: Present and Past

 Review and Integration: Present, Past, Present Perfect

1.

2. ask, asking **3.** begin, begins **4.** bites, biting **5.** buys, buying **6.** come, comes **7.** digs, digging **8.** do, doing **9.** employ, employs **10.** fly, flies **11.** forgets, forgetting **12.** have, having **13.** lie, lies **14.** manages, managing **15.** promise, promises **16.** say, saying **17.** studies, studying **18.** travel, travels **19.** uses, using **20.** write, writing

2.

2. doesn't know **3.** 's concentrating **4.** 's writing **5.** 's giving **6.** studies **7.** believe **8.** write **9.** tells **10.** 'm beginning **11.** don't take **12.** finds **13.** asks **14.** 'm walking **15.** says **16.** doesn't remember **17.** knows **18.** use **19.** tells **20.** is handing **21.** does . . . hope/is . . . hoping **22.** wants **23.** 'm looking **24.** 'm examining **25.** indicates **26.** is going **27.** 's handling **28.** 's not confiding/isn't confiding **29.** shows **30.** represents **31.** is planning **32.** doesn't leave **33.** avoids **34.** tell **35.** 're reading **36.** is investigating **37.** display **38.** emphasizes **39.** takes **40.** warns **41.** doesn't guarantee

3.

2. apply **3.** was/were **4.** became **5.** described **6.** developed **7.** eat **8.** got **9.** grew **10.** invented **11.** lived **12.** pay **13.** permitted **14.** planned **15.** send **16.** slept

4.

2. signed **3.** didn't know **4.** was **5.** became **6.** was/is **7.** wanted **8.** was living **9.** sent **10.** admitted **11.** loved **12.** died **13.** became **14.** used **15.** was inspecting **16.** pushed **17.** nailed **18.** named **19.** was going to marry **20.** went **21.** was hiding **22.** began **23.** wrote **24.** was serving **25.** started **26.** was **27.** was going to appoint **28.** ran away **29.** was developing **30.** invented **31.** began **32.** broke out **33.** moved **34.** boarded **35.** was traveling **36.** fired

5.

2. brought, brought **3.** chose, chosen **4.** delayed, delayed **5.** felt, felt **6.** found, found **7.** finished, finished **8.** got, gotten **9.** graduated, graduated **10.** hid, hidden **11.** moved, moved **12.** noticed, noticed **13.** owned, owned **14.** read, read **15.** replied, replied **16.** ripped, ripped **17.** showed, shown **18.** spoke, spoken **19.** threw, thrown **20.** wondered, wondered

6.

2. She graduated from college in 1990. **3.** She's been reporting/'s reported crime news since 1993. **4.** Recently, she's been researching articles about crime in schools. **5.** Her father worked for the Broadfield Police Department for twenty years. **6.** Simon Pohlig moved to Broadfield in 1988. **7.** He's owned Sharney's Restaurant since 1990. **8.** He's written two cookbooks for children. **9.** He's been planning a local television show for several months. **10.** The groom's mother has been serving/has served as president of TLC Meals, Inc. for two years.

7.

2. 's working/works **3.** 's covering/covers **4.** doesn't want **5.** was drinking . . . was making out **6.** spilled . . . was writing **7.** was going to write/wrote **8.** remembered . . . squeezed **9.** 's been working/'s worked **10.** found . . . was attending **11.** lived **12.** 's living/lives **13.** moved . . . got **14.** was going to get . . . changed **15.** was studying . . . decided **16.** graduated **17.** hasn't received **18.** shows/showed **19.** left . . . mentioned **20.** wasn't telling/didn't tell **21.** doesn't want **22.** connected/connects . . . didn't slant/doesn't slant **23.** indicate **24.** seems **25.** suggest

UNIT 2 Past Perfect

1.

3. entertained 4. cut 5. told 6. withdraw 7. practiced
8. worried 9. seek 10. swept 11. quit 12. led 13. write
14. stolen 15. planned 16. break 17. swum 18. bet
19. sink 20. forgiven

2.

2. had enjoyed 3. had become 4. had started 5. had . . .
invented 6. hadn't appreciated 7. had written 8. had been
9. had seen 10. hadn't done 11. had gotten
12. hadn't been 13. had grown 14. hadn't seen 15. had
made 16. had come

3.

2. Had he driven   No, he hadn't. 3. Had he arrived
No, he hadn't. 4. Had he gone   Yes, he had. 5. Had he
worked   Yes, he had. 6. Had he met   No, he hadn't.

7. Had he taped   Yes, he had. 8. Had he had/eaten   No,
he hadn't. 9. Had he had/eaten   Yes, he had. 10. Had he
gone   Yes, he had.

4.

2. Before he appeared in New York comedy clubs, he had
gotten a part-time job as a car mechanic. 3. He wrote for
TV after he had moved to Los Angeles. 4. By the time he
appeared on "The Tonight Show," he had written for the TV
show "Good Times." 5. He had appeared on "The Tonight
Show" before he appeared on "Late Night with David
Letterman." 6. When he got married, he had already
appeared on "Late Night with David Letterman." 7. By the
time he did his first prime-time TV show, he had played at
Carnegie Hall. 8. He had had a TV comedy special by the
time he did his first prime-time TV show. 9. He had
appeared on "The Tonight Show" many times when he
became the permanent host of "The Tonight Show."

UNIT 3 Past Perfect Progressive

1.

2. 'd been keeping 3. had been waiting 4. holding back
5. had been talking to 6. had been running 7. had been
shouting 8. had been raining 9. had been galloping
10. had been competing

2.

2.a. Had . . . been expecting b. No, I hadn't. 3.a. had . . .
been behaving 4.a. Had . . . been worrying b. Yes, I had.
5.a. had . . . been hesitating 6.a. Had . . . been considering
b. Yes, I had 7.a. Had . . . been anticipating b. No, I hadn't.

3.

2. By the time Julie turned three years old, she'd already
been riding for a year. 3. Her mother had only been
teaching her for a year before Julie won first prize in a state
fair. 4. Julie hadn't been thinking about becoming a jockey
for very long when she got her first job as a professional.
5. When she entered her first race as a professional, Julie
hadn't been living with her parents for several months.
6. She hadn't been racing for even two months before she
won her first professional race. 7. By the time she
completed her first year as a professional, she hadn't been
attending high school for more than a year. 8. Julie had
been competing professionally for less than two years when
she won a prize for best jockey at a famous track. 9. She'd
been earning half a million dollars a year by the time she
won at Belmont. 10. Before she won first prize there, Julie
had been losing at Belmont for two years.

PART II: Future

UNIT 4 Future Progressive

1.

2. will be living 3. will be parking 4. won't be preparing
5. will be eating 6. won't be driving 7. will be relocating
8. will . . . be saving 9. won't be buying 10. won't be paying

11. won't be worrying 12. will be providing 13. will be
attending 14. will be seeing

2.

2. will you be using the lawn mower tomorrow? No, I won't.
3. When will we be getting new washers? 4. will you be going to the post office tomorrow? Yes, I will. 5. What will you be making? 6. Who will be watching the kids tomorrow? 7. Will the entertainment committee be planning anything else in the near future? Yes, we will.
8. Will we be meeting every month? Yes, we will.
9. Will we still be meeting then? No, we won't.

3.

2. will be meeting with . . . faxes reports 3. attends . . . will be having a phone conference with John Smith
4. has/eats . . . will be having/eating lunch with Jack Allen
5. will be billing clients . . . drafts 6. picks up . . . will be taking Amanda to the dentist 7. will be shopping for . . . takes Tommy to the barber 8. pays . . . will be cutting the grass

 Future Perfect and Future Perfect Progressive

1.

2. will have completed 3. will have helped 4. will have been using 5. 'll have bought 6. 'll have wrapped 7. won't have planned 8. won't have decided 9. 'll . . . have been arguing 10. won't have wasted 11. 'll have completed
12. 'll have had 13. 'll have participated 14. will have redecorated 15. 'll have made 16. 'll . . . have done
17. 'll have straightened 18. 'll have packed 19. 'll have been explaining

2.

1. Yes, I will. 2. will . . . have been singing 3. will . . . have sewn 4. will . . . have been waiting 5. will . . . have dried No, it won't. 6. Will . . . have delivered Yes, they will.
7. will . . . have been living/have lived

3.

2. A: How long will Aida have been walking by August 31?
B: She'll have been walking for a month. 3. A: How many rooms will Arnie have painted by August 5? B: He'll have painted three rooms. 4. A: How long will Arnie have been painting by August 15? B: He'll have been painting for two weeks. 5. A: On August 16, will Arnie have left for his dentist appointment by four o'clock? B: Yes, he will.
6. A: Will Aida have unpacked all the fall clothing by August 23? B: No, she won't. 7. A: How long will Aida have been driving in the carpool by August 19? B: She'll have been driving in the carpool for two weeks. 8. A: How many quarts of blueberries will Corrie have picked by August 19? B: She'll have picked three quarts of blueberries.
9. A: How many pies will Aida and Corrie have baked by August 21? B: They'll have baked six pies. 10. A: Will they have finished packing for the trip by August 31? B: Yes, they will. 11. A: How long will the family have been traveling when they arrive at Mom and Dad's? B: They'll have been traveling for three days. 12. A: Will they have had their picnic by September 3? B: No, they won't.

PART III: Tag Questions, Additions, and Responses

 **Tag Questions**

1.

2. doesn't it? No, it doesn't. 3. is it? No, it isn't.
4. haven't you? Yes, I have. 5. does it? Yes, it does.
6. didn't you? Yes, I did. 7. isn't there? Yes, there is.
8. can I? Yes, you can. 9. will you? No, I won't.
10. don't you? Yes, I do.

2.

1.c. 's 2.a. haven't seen b. didn't you c. shouldn't it
3.a. isn't there b. didn't there c. hadn't been 4.a. aren't they b. have you c. can take

3.

3. This is a good building, isn't it? 4. The owner takes good care of it, doesn't he? 5. He recently redid the lobby, didn't he? 6. He doesn't talk very much, does he? 7. The rent won't increase next year, will it? 8. All the apartments aren't occupied, are they? 9. Some new people will be moving into apartment 1B, won't they? 10. This is really a nice place to live, isn't it?

Additions and Responses with *So, Too, Neither, Not either,* and *But*

1.

2. has **3.** did **4.** but **5.** neither **6.** are **7.** either **8.** do **9.** will **10.** too **11.** don't **12.** so

2.

2. did too **3.** neither does **4.** so did **5.** couldn't either **6.** but . . . didn't **7.** so is **8.** hasn't either **9.** but . . . don't

3.

2. but fish shouldn't **3.** and so must dogs/and dogs must too **4.** and neither do fish/and fish don't either **5.** but birds and fish don't **6.** but a fish doesn't **7.** and so can a fish/and a fish can too **8.** and so will some fish/and some fish will too **9.** but other pets don't **10.** and neither do fish/and fish don't either **11.** and so do cats/and cats do too **12.** and neither do birds/and birds don't either

PART IV: Gerunds and Infinitives

Gerunds and Infinitives: Review and Expansion

1.

2. to provide **3.** Overhauling **4.** to convince/convincing **5.** to adopt **6.** to do **7.** to curb **8.** censoring **9.** to help **10.** perform/to perform **11.** to begin **12.** to learn **13.** changing **14.** to alter **15.** regulating/to regulate **16.** not to turn on **17.** not to respond **18.** to update **19.** to take **20.** to use **21.** taking **22.** Redoing **23.** to listen **24.** to change **25.** to expect **26.** to rate **27.** to warn **28.** selling **29.** to take **30.** to face **31.** to impose

2.

2. unwilling to change **3.** used to putting **4.** fed up with seeing **5.** likely to hit **6.** force . . . to rate **7.** hesitate to tell

8. decided to run **9.** stopped showing **10.** dislike turning off **11.** insist on changing **12.** forbid turning on **13.** permit tuning in **14.** dream of owning

3.

2. A V-chip interferes with their/them watching violent shows. **3.** Beakman encourages them to send in questions. **4.** The father objected to Jennifer's/Jennifer watching cop shows. **5.** The teacher recommended their watching "Nick News." **6.** Bob didn't remember their/them seeing that game. **7.** Sharif's parents persuaded him not to watch "Z-Men." **8.** The mother insisted on Sara's/Sara turning off the TV. **9.** Aziza wanted Ben to change the channel. **10.** Paul can't understand Nick's/Nick watching the show.

Verbs Followed by Objects and the Base Form: *Make, Have, Let, Help*

1.

2. made **3.** let **4.** made **5.** let **6.** got **7.** helped **8.** had **9.** made **10.** have **11.** made **12.** let **13.** made

2.

2. didn't let them take **3.** had them answer **4.** made them hand in **5.** didn't let them submit **6.** had them write **7.** let them come **8.** had them submit **9.** made them sign **10.** had them keep **11.** didn't make them go **12.** help them do/to do

3.

2. made Mark/him work it out himself **3.** let students/them come by for help **4.** made Sara/her try again **5.** had Robert/him do his homework/it over **6.** didn't let the students/them use a calculator **7.** got the students/them to help clean up the classroom **8.** had Ken/him describe the process to her

PART V: Passive

UNIT 10 The Passive: Overview

1.

3. Alice and Jay were fired. 4. The copies were delivered yesterday. 5. Al Baker wrote the article. 6. They frequently hire new editors. 7. The new editor was interviewed by Marla Jacobson. 8. They gave Marla an assignment on the Philippines.

2.

2. were called 3. is known 4. are made up 5. are considered 6. were formed 7. were not given 8. are called

3.

3. are inhabited 4. are found 5. damage 6. cause 7. was covered 8. cover 9. contain 10. are found 11. are used 12. are known

4.

3. were followed by groups from Indonesia 4. are spoken 5. is understood by speakers of another dialect 6. was declared by President Manuel Quezon 7. was spoken by 55 percent of the Filipinos 8. is spoken by 43 million people 9. is spoken 10. is used

5.

2. What other minerals are mined? Gold and silver. 3. Where are fruits and nuts grown? In the north/northeast and in the central part of the country. 4. Are llamas found in the east? No, they aren't. 5. Where is logging done? In the east. 6. What animals are raised? Sheep, cattle, and llamas. 7. Are potatoes grown? Yes, they are. 8. Where is rubber produced? In the north.

UNIT 11 The Passive with Modals

1.

2. Some new airports will be constructed on islands. 3. They might put passenger facilities on decks under the runways. 4. A lot of space could be saved that way. 5. Japan will build a new airport in Osaka Bay. 6. An artificial island has to be created for the airport. 7. They have got to move huge amounts of earth from nearby mountains. 8. An island airport will also be built by Hong Kong. 9. They can't reach the island right now except by boat. 10. Airport planners must provide bridges and tunnels.

2.

2. can be linked 3. may be launched 4. will be completed 5. are going to be connected 6. will be carried 7. will not be permitted 8. are going to be transported 9. may be joined 10. could be spanned 11. have to be developed 12. must be spanned 13. will be built 14. will be included 15. might not be fulfilled 16. can't be avoided 17. will be solved

3.

2. No, they can't. 3. Must . . . be accompanied 4. Yes, they must. 5. Will . . . be required 6. No, they won't. 7. Is . . . going to be provided 8. No, it isn't. 9. Can . . . be made 10. No, they can't. 11. Could . . . be delayed 12. Yes, it could.

UNIT 12 Passive Causatives

1.

2. I'm having/getting my house painted. 3. I had/got my car checked last month. 4. We've just had/gotten our windows cleaned. 5. We must have/get our repairs done. 6. We're going to have/get our roof fixed. 7. I'll have/get my hair cut by Marie. 8. We should have/get our electric wiring checked.

2.

2. have . . . completed 3. have . . . done 4. get . . . tested 5. have . . . replaced 6. have . . . investigated 7. had . . . installed 8. get . . . replaced 9. didn't have . . . done 10. had . . . tested 11. have . . . checked out 12. have . . . stopped 13. have . . . put 14. getting . . . publicized

3.

2. How often do you get it done? **3.** Did you get it winterized? **4.** Have you ever gotten snow tires put on? **5.** Are you going to get/Will you get/Are you getting snow tires put on for the trip? **6.** How often have you gotten it checked since then? **7.** Why do you get it done there?

4.

2. He didn't have/get the oil changed. **3.** He didn't have/get the undercarriage inspected. **4.** He had/got the body and chassis lubricated. **5.** He had/got the air filter inspected. **6.** He didn't have/get the air filter replaced. **7.** He didn't have/get the tires rotated. **8.** He didn't have/get the timing and engine speed adjusted. **9.** He had/got the automatic transmission serviced. **10.** He had/got the cooling system flushed.

TEST: UNITS 1–3

PART ONE

DIRECTIONS: Circle the letter of the correct answer to complete each sentence.

Example:

Mark _____ a headache last night.   Ⓐ   **B**   **C**   **D**

   A. had

   B. has

   C. has had

   D. was having

1. Her name is Victoria, but her friends _____   **A**   **B**   **C**   **D**

   her Vicki.

   A. are calling

   B. call

   C. had called

   D. were calling

2. Water _____ at 0 degrees C.   **A**   **B**   **C**   **D**

   A. freezes

   B. froze

   C. has been freezing

   D. is freezing

3. In her latest book, the author _____   **A**   **B**   **C**   **D**

   her childhood.

   A. describes

   B. is describing

   C. has been describing

   D. was describing

4. John _____. It really annoys me.   A   B   C   D

A. always complain

B. had always complained

C. is always complaining

D. was always complaining

5. I _____ Jackie, but I didn't.   A   B   C   D

A. told

B. 've told

C. was going to tell

D. was telling

6. By 11:00 this morning, I _____   A   B   C   D

three cups of coffee.

A. drink

B. had been drinking

C. had drunk

D. have drunk

7. I was listening to the radio when I _____   A   B   C   D

the news.

A. hear

B. heard

C. 've heard

D. was hearing

8. They _____ in Paris when they   A   B   C   D

met for the first time.

A. lived

B. 've lived

C. 've been living

D. were living

9. Sara always _____ glasses. She can't see

without them.

A. had worn

B. has been wearing

C. is wearing

D. wears

A   B   C   D

10. Can you please turn down the radio? The

baby _____.

A. has slept

B. is sleeping

C. sleeps

D. slept

A   B   C   D

11. The Morrisons _____ to Texas

last September.

A. had moved

B. have been moving

C. have moved

D. moved

A   B   C   D

12. While Jedd was living in Toronto, Helen _____

in California.

A. has lived

B. had lived

C. lives

D. was living

A   B   C   D

PART TWO

DIRECTIONS: Each sentence has four underlined words or phrases. The four underlined parts of the sentence are marked A, B, C, or D. Circle the letter of the one underlined word or phrase that is NOT CORRECT.

Example:

Rosa <u>rarely</u> <u>is using</u> public transportation, but <u>this morning</u>
     A   B   C

she <u>is taking</u> the bus.
   D

                                  A   Ⓑ   **C**   **D**

13. The doctor <u>called</u> <u>this morning</u> <u>while</u> you <u>slept</u>.
            A   B   C   D

      A   **B**   **C**   **D**

14. <u>When</u> she <u>was</u> little, they <u>were naming</u> her
   A   B   C

    "Strawberry" because she <u>had</u> beautiful red hair.
                           D

      A   **B**   **C**   **D**

15. They <u>were going to</u> <u>drive</u> to the beach, but they
          A   B

    <u>have changed</u> their plans when it <u>started</u> to rain.
        C   D

      A   **B**   **C**   **D**

16. <u>By the time</u> I <u>had gotten</u> home, the show <u>had</u>
     A   B   C

    <u>already ended</u>.
       D

      A   **B**   **C**   **D**

17. Pete and Andy <u>were</u> <u>driving</u> to work <u>when</u> they
              A   B   C

    <u>were seeing</u> the accident.
       D

      A   **B**   **C**   **D**

18. Erika <u>has</u> <u>been looking</u> for a job <u>since</u> she
       A   B   C

    <u>has graduated</u> from college.
       D

      A   **B**   **C**   **D**

19. Janice <u>didn't own</u> a car then because she <u>hasn't</u>
         A   B

    <u>learned</u> to drive <u>yet</u>.
     C   D

      A   **B**   **C**   **D**

20. I <u>had</u> <u>been living</u> in this apartment for ten years,
     A   B

    but <u>I'm</u> <u>looking</u> for a new one now.
        C   D

      A   **B**   **C**   **D**

TEST: UNITS 4–5

PART ONE

DIRECTIONS: Circle the letter of the correct answer to complete each sentence.

Example:

Mark _____ a headache last night.   Ⓐ   **B**   **C**   **D**

  A. had

  B. has

  C. has had

  D. was having

1. Bill will be _____ to Taipei tomorrow.   **A**   **B**   **C**   **D**

  A. flies

  B. flying

  C. fly

  D. have been flying

2. We _____ a new TV soon.   **A**   **B**   **C**   **D**

  A. had owned

  B. 'll own

  C. 're owning

  D. 've owned

3. _____ you be driving into the city next week?   **A**   **B**   **C**   **D**

  A. Are

  B. Did

  C. Have

  D. Will

4. They'll be making photocopies while he   **A**   **B**   **C**   **D**

_____ typing the report.

A. finishes

B. 'll be finishing

C. 'll finish

D. 's been finishing

5. I _____ be working tomorrow.   **A**   **B**   **C**   **D**

I'll be out of town.

A. don't

B. haven't

C. 'm not

D. won't

6. Kareem will _____ almost $1,000 by next year.   **A**   **B**   **C**   **D**

A. had saved

B. have been saving

C. have saved

D. saves

7. We're late. When we _____ there,   **A**   **B**   **C**   **D**

they'll already have eaten dinner.

A. get

B. got

C. 'll get

D. 'll have gotten

8. By the end of this week, Henry _____

     regularly for six months.

  A. exercised

  B. exercises

  C. will exercise

  D. will have been exercising

A   B   C   D

9. When I finish this mystery story by Nguyen Treng, I'll

     _____ all of her mysteries.

  A. be reading

  B. have been reading

  C. have read

  D. read

A   B   C   D

10. Next year, the Carters will have been living in that house

     _____ forty years.

  A. already

  B. for

  C. since

  D. yet

A   B   C   D

PART TWO

DIRECTIONS: Each sentence has four underlined words or phrases. The four underlined parts of the sentence are marked A, B, C, or D. Circle the letter of the one underlined word or phrase that is NOT CORRECT.

Example:

Rosa <u>rarely</u> <u>is using</u> public transportation, but
    A   B

<u>this morning</u> she <u>is taking</u> the bus.
   C   D

A   Ⓑ   C   D

11. <u>Will</u> you <u>been</u> <u>going</u> to the drugstore <u>tonight</u>?
    A   B   C   D

A   B   C   D

12. While Bill <u>will wash</u> the dishes, <u>I'll</u> be <u>straightening</u>
    A   B   C   D
the living room.

                                            A   B   C   D

13. <u>After</u> I <u>finished</u> this lap, <u>I'll have</u> <u>walked</u> three miles.
    A   B   C   D

                                            A   B   C   D

14. What time <u>will</u> Professor Sanek <u>be</u> <u>arrives</u> <u>today</u>?
               A   B   C   D

                                            A   B   C   D

15. The Tokagarus <u>will save</u> <u>for</u> ten years <u>by the time</u>
                   A   B   C
their children <u>enter</u> college.
               D

                                            A   B   C   D

16. Seana will <u>has</u> <u>been</u> watching television <u>for</u> an hour
                A   B   C
by the time dinner <u>is</u> ready.
                    D

                                            A   B   C   D

17. In the twenty-first century, most <u>people</u> in this
                                       A
country <u>will</u> <u>be</u> <u>work</u> in service jobs.
          B   C   D

                                            A   B   C   D

18. At the end of this year, Tania <u>will</u> <u>have</u> been <u>paying</u>
                                 A   B   C
her credit card bill <u>since</u> three years.
                        D

                                            A   B   C   D

19. She<u>'ll</u> <u>have</u> <u>been paying</u> a total of $3,000 by the time
        A   B   C
she <u>pays off</u> her loan.
         D

                                            A   B   C   D

20. John loves that old suitcase. By the time he <u>gets</u> home
                                           A
from vacation <u>next month</u>, he'll <u>have</u> <u>carries</u> it at least
               B   C   D
50,000 miles.

TEST: UNITS 6–7

PART ONE

DIRECTIONS: Circle the letter of the correct answer to complete each sentence.

Example:

Mark _____ a headache last night.   Ⓐ   **B**   **C**   **D**

A. had

B. has

C. has had

D. was having

1. You're from Panama, _____?   **A**   **B**   **C**   **D**

A. are you

B. aren't you

C. you are

D. you aren't

2. Ben's not at work today, _____?   **A**   **B**   **C**   **D**

A. does he

B. doesn't he

C. is he

D. isn't he

3. Your cousin lived in New York, _____?   **A**   **B**   **C**   **D**

A. didn't she

B. hadn't she

C. isn't she

D. wasn't she

4. Miguel _____ here very long, has he?   **A**   **B**   **C**   **D**

A. has been

B. hasn't been

C. was

D. wasn't

5. The Millers _____ a house in Florida,   **A**   **B**   **C**   **D**

don't they?

A. do

B. don't own

C. own

D. owns

6. Rick can't speak Spanish, _____?   **A**   **B**   **C**   **D**

A. can he

B. does he

C. is he

D. is he able

7. That's your notebook, isn't _____?   **A**   **B**   **C**   **D**

A. he

B. it

C. she

D. that

8. A: You're not Alex, are you?

B: _____ I'm Alex Winslow.   **A**   **B**   **C**   **D**

A. No, I'm not.

B. No, you're not.

C. Yes, I am.

D. Yes, you are.

9. A: Today's July 5th, isn't it?　　　　　　　　　　　　**A　　B　　C　　D**

    B: _____ It's the 6th.

A. Neither is it.

B. No, it isn't.

C. So is it.

D. Yes, it is.

10. They've read the paper, _____ I have too.　　**A　　B　　C　　D**

A. and

B. but

C. either

D. neither

11. A: Jennifer ate at home last night.　　　　　　　　　　**A　　B　　C　　D**

    B: _____ I saw him having dinner in the

school cafeteria.

A. But Mike did.

B. But Mike didn't.

C. Neither did Mike.

D. So did Mike.

12. A: Andrea speaks fluent French.　　　　　　　　　　　**A　　B　　C　　D**

    B: _____

A. Neither does Paul.

B. So does Paul.

C. So is Paul.

D. So Paul does.

13. A: The Mets played well last night.   A   B   C   D

    B: So _____ the Phillies. It was

       an exciting game.

A. did

B. didn't

C. played

D. were

14. The hotel _____ expensive, and so were   A   B   C   D

   the restaurants.

A. was

B. wasn't

C. were

D. weren't

PART TWO

DIRECTIONS: Each sentence has four underlined words or phrases. The four underlined parts of the sentence are marked A, B, C, or D. Circle the letter of the <u>one</u> underlined word or phrase that is NOT CORRECT.

Example:

Rosa <u>rarely</u> <u>is using</u> public transportation, but   A   Ⓑ   C   D
     A   B

<u>this morning</u> she <u>is taking</u> the bus.
   C   D

15. <u>This</u> <u>isn't</u> the way to Route 101, <u>is</u> <u>this</u>?   A   B   C   D
    A   B   C D

16. Mary <u>works</u> on Saturdays<u>,</u> <u>doesn't</u> <u>Mary</u>?   A   B   C   D
       A   B   C   D

17. Jeff <u>bought</u> a new car, <u>and</u> <u>so</u> <u>does</u> Ann.   A   B   C   D
      A   B C D

18. Rachel <u>didn't</u> <u>go</u> to class today, <u>and</u> her sister <u>did</u>.   A   B   C   D
        A   B   C   D

19. I <u>didn't enjoy</u> the movie, <u>and</u> Frank <u>did</u> <u>either</u>.   A   B   C   D
      A   B   C D

20. Vilma <u>is coming</u> to the party, <u>and</u> <u>so</u> <u>Craig is</u>.   A   B   C   D
        A   B C   D

TEST: UNITS 8–9

PART ONE

DIRECTIONS: Circle the letter of the correct answer to complete each sentence.

Example:

Mark _____ a headache last night.   Ⓐ   **B**   **C**   **D**

  A. had

  B. has

  C. has had

  D. was having

1. _____ the streets safe again is the mayor's   **A**   **B**   **C**   **D**

  highest priority.

  A. Is making

  B. Make

  C. Makes

  D. Making

2. Geraldo is looking forward to _____ a father.   **A**   **B**   **C**   **D**

  A. became

  B. become

  C. becomes

  D. becoming

3. It was very difficult _____ a good job.   **A**   **B**   **C**   **D**

  A. find

  B. found

  C. has found

  D. to find

4. Elliot bought an exercise video _____   **A**   **B**   **C**   **D**

him get into shape.

A. helped

B. helps

C. is helping

D. to help

5. It's time _____ where we want to go   **A**   **B**   **C**   **D**

this summer.

A. decide

B. decides

C. deciding

D. to decide

6. I'm sorry, but I forgot _____ that book   **A**   **B**   **C**   **D**

you asked for.

A. bring

B. bringing

C. brought

D. to bring

7. I can't imagine _____ that.   **A**   **B**   **C**   **D**

A. do

B. to do

C. you to do

D. your doing

8. Pat invited _____ the weekend with them.   **A**   **B**   **C**   **D**

A. I spend

B. me spend

C. me to spend

D. my spending

9. The judge made the witness _____   A   B   C   D

the question.

A. answer

B. answered

C. answering

D. to answer

10. It's a good idea _____ a reservation.   A   B   C   D

A. make

B. makes

C. made

D. to make

11. The defendant denied _____ a weapon.   A   B   C   D

A. owned

B. owning

C. owns

D. to own

12. Gary was busy, and he didn't remember _____.   A   B   C   D

A. studied

B. studies

C. studying

D. to study

PART TWO

DIRECTIONS: Each sentence has four underlined words or phrases. The four underlined parts of the sentence are marked A, B, C, or D. Circle the letter of the <u>one</u> underlined word or phrase that is NOT CORRECT.

Example:

Rosa <u>rarely</u> <u>is using</u> public transportation, but
     A   B

<u>this morning</u> she <u>is taking</u> the bus.
    C   D

                                                           A   **Ⓑ**   **C**   **D**

13. I <u>got</u> all my friends <u>help</u> <u>me</u> <u>move</u> last June.   **A**   **B**   **C**   **D**
      A   B   C   D

14. Phil decided <u>changing</u> jobs because his boss   **A**   **B**   **C**   **D**
                  A

always <u>made</u> <u>him</u> <u>work</u> overtime.
        B   C   D

15. The students of Maitlin High <u>appreciated</u> their <u>principal's</u>   **A**   **B**   **C**   **D**
                            A   B

<u>try</u> <u>to improve</u> conditions in their school.
 C   D

16. Sally is really tired <u>for</u> <u>being</u> responsible for   **A**   **B**   **C**   **D**
                    A   B

<u>everyone's</u> <u>doing</u> the work on time.
   C   D

17. Robert <u>succeeded in</u> <u>to find</u> a job after high school,   **A**   **B**   **C**   **D**
            A   B

so his parents <u>didn't make</u> him <u>apply</u> to college.
               C   D

18. If you insist <u>on</u> <u>looking</u> over the report, please   **A**   **B**   **C**   **D**
              A   B

<u>don't forget</u> <u>returning</u> it by Monday.
   C   D

19. <u>Going</u> on a diet doesn't <u>seem</u> <u>to be</u> the best way   **A**   **B**   **C**   **D**
   A   B   C

<u>losing</u> weight.
  D

20. If you're <u>planning</u> <u>to be</u> near the post office today,   **A**   **B**   **C**   **D**
           A   B

<u>could</u> you stop <u>buying</u> some stamps?
  C   D

TEST: UNITS 10–12

PART ONE

DIRECTIONS: Circle the letter of the correct answer to complete each sentence.

Example:

Mark _____ a headache last night.   Ⓐ   B   C   D

  A. had

  B. has

  C. has had

  D. was having

1. That novel was written _____ Amy Tan.   A   B   C   D

A. at

B. by

C. from

D. to

2. A: Do you cut your own hair?   A   B   C   D

   B: No. I _____.

A. cut it

B. have cut it

C. have it cut

D. haven't

3. This magazine _____ by many people.   A   B   C   D

A. are read

B. is read

C. is reading

D. reads

4. _____ these books published in Europe?   **A   B   C   D**

A. Do

B. Have

C. Was

D. Were

5. A: When _____ it built?   **A   B   C   D**

   B: In 1960.

A. does

B. has

C. is

D. was

6. Cotton _____ in the southern part   **A   B   C   D**

   of the country.

A. is produced

B. is producing

C. produced

D. produces

7. The project _____ soon.   **A   B   C   D**

A. finishes

B. is finished

C. will be finished

D. will finish

8. A: When will the work be completed?

   B: It _____ be done by June, but I'm not

     really sure.

    A. has

    B. might

    C. will

    D. won't

       A   B   C   D

9. How often _____ your car serviced since

   you bought it?

    A. do you get

    B. did you get

    C. had you gotten

    D. have you gotten

       A   B   C   D

10. I think she usually _____ her own clothes.

    A. have made

    B. has them made

    C. is made

    D. makes

       A   B   C   D

PART TWO

DIRECTIONS: Each sentence has four underlined words or phrases. The four underlined parts of the sentence are marked A, B, C, or D. Circle the letter of the <u>one</u> underlined word or phrase that is NOT CORRECT.

Example:

Rosa <u>rarely</u> <u>is using</u> public transportation, but <u>this morning</u>
   A   B   C

she <u>is taking</u> the bus.
   D

       A   Ⓑ   C   D

11. That movie <u>was</u> <u>directed</u> <u>from</u> <u>someone</u> very well known.
           A   B   C   D

       A   B   C   D

12. Before a final decision <u>is reached</u>, it <u>should</u>
A B

    <u>discussed</u> <u>by</u> the whole team.
C D

                                            A   **B**   **C**   **D**

13. I <u>used to</u> do my own taxes, <u>but</u> now I
 A   B

    <u>have done them</u> <u>by</u> an accountant.
      C   D

                                            A   **B**   **C**   **D**

14. The house <u>painted</u> three years ago, but I'm not
          A

    <u>going to</u> <u>have</u> <u>it done</u> again for a while.
      B   C   D

                                            A   **B**   **C**   **D**

15. We <u>didn't</u> <u>know</u> about the problem so it <u>shouldn't</u>
     A   B   C

    <u>be avoided</u>.
     D

                                            A   **B**   **C**   **D**

16. A lot of crops <u>can't</u> be <u>grew</u> in the mountains
               A   B

    because <u>it</u> <u>gets</u> too cold.
         C   D

                                            A   **B**   **C**   **D**

17. That pottery <u>was</u> <u>found</u> <u>by</u> an archaeologist while
             A   B   C

    she <u>was worked</u> in this area.
        D

                                            A   **B**   **C**   **D**

18. When we <u>visit</u> Mexico, we<u>'re going to</u> <u>have</u> our
        A   B   C

    pictures <u>took</u> on top of an Aztec temple.
         D

                                            A   **B**   **C**   **D**

19. You <u>should</u> <u>be get</u> the locks <u>changed</u> after you
       A   B   C

    <u>move</u> into a new apartment.
     D

                                            A   **B**   **C**   **D**

20. <u>When</u> it <u>is launched</u>, the new space station <u>will</u>
     A   B   C

    <u>be carried</u> an international crew.
     D

                                            A   **B**   **C**   **D**

ANSWER KEY FOR TEST: UNITS 1–3

Note: Correct responses for Part Two questions appear in parentheses.

PART ONE

1. B **2.** A **3.** A **4.** C **5.** C **6.** C **7.** B **8.** D **9.** D **10.** B **11.** D **12.** D

PART TWO

13. D (were sleeping) **14.** C (named) **15.** C (changed) **16.** B (got) **17.** D (saw) **18.** D (graduated)
19. B (hadn't) **20.** A (have)

ANSWER KEY FOR TEST: UNITS 4–5

PART ONE

1. B **2.** B **3.** D **4.** A **5.** D **6.** C **7.** A **8.** D **9.** C **10.** B

PART TWO

11. B (be) **12.** B (washes) **13.** B (finish) **14.** C (arriving) **15.** A (will have been saving) **16.** A (have)
17. D (working) **18.** D (for) **19.** C (paid) **20.** D (carried)

ANSWER KEY FOR TEST: UNITS 6–7

PART ONE

1. B **2.** C **3.** A **4.** B **5.** C **6.** A **7.** B **8.** C **9.** B **10.** A **11.** B **12.** B **13.** A **14.** A

PART TWO

15. D (it) **16.** D (she) **17.** D (did) **18.** C (but) **19.** C (didn't) **20.** D (is Craig)

ANSWER KEY FOR TEST: UNITS 8–9

PART ONE

1. D **2.** D **3.** D **4.** D **5.** D **6.** D **7.** D **8.** C **9.** A **10.** D **11.** C **12.** D

PART TWO

13. B (to help) **14.** A (to change) **15.** C (trying) **16.** A (of) **17.** B (finding) **18.** D (to return)
19. D (of losing/to lose) **20.** D (to buy)

ANSWER KEY FOR TEST: UNITS 10–12

PART ONE

1. B   **2.** C   **3.** B   **4.** D   **5.** D   **6.** A   **7.** C   **8.** B   **9.** D   **10.** D

PART TWO

11. C (by)   **12.** C (be discussed)   **13.** C (have them done)   **14.** A (was painted)   **15.** C (couldn't)
16. B (grown)   **17.** D (was working/worked)   **18.** D (taken)   **19.** B (get)   **20.** D (carry)